THE POWER PIVOT

THE POWER PIVOT

WITH GRIT, GRACE, AND GROWTH

ASHLEY DAVIS

A POST HILL PRESS BOOK
ISBN: 979-8-89565-406-4
ISBN (eBook): 979-8-89565-407-1

The Power Pivot:
With Grit, Grace, and Growth

Cover design by Conroy Accord

This book, as well as any other Post Hill Press publications, may be purchased in bulk quantities at a special discounted rate. Contact orders@posthillpress.com for more information.

Post Hill Press
New York • Nashville
posthillpress.com

Published in the United States of America
2 3 4 5 6 7 8 9 10

For Mom, Dad, Oliver, and Joel

TABLE OF CONTENTS

Introduction...XI

Chapter 1: The Value of Small Pivots 1
Chapter 2: Embracing the Process 9
Chapter 3: In the Beginning.. 15

The Power Pivot: Personal

Chapter 4: Being Intentional..29
Chapter 5: The Power Pivot: The Framework for
Personal Success..35
Chapter 6: How to Start the Power Pivot 43

The Power Pivot: Business

Chapter 7: The Power Pivot for Business 49
Chapter 8: The Three Pillars of Executing 53
Chapter 9: Introduction to the Power Pivot Blueprint..........63

The Power Pivot: Leadership

Chapter 10: Good Leaders Pivot 71

Chapter 11: Deepening the Framework: Why Good Leaders Must Pivot 79

The Power Pivot: The Time is Now

Chapter 12: Tiny Pivots 89
Chapter 13: How Tiny Pivots Lead to Big Transformation 97
Chapter 14: Strategic Tiny Pivots Drive Lasting Leadership Change 105
Epilogue: The Art of the Power Pivot: Embracing Change with Purpose and Vision 113

Acknowledgments 121

INTRODUCTION

Tick. Tick. Tick. Tick.

The monotonous staccato of the government-issued wall clock was about the only thing breaking up the quietness of the West Wing basement that morning. The ceilings were low, but the walls were densely adorned, giving it a curated feel. Photos of President George W. Bush, my boss, posing at various events dotted the otherwise austere walls. The catacombs of the White House under the North Portico didn't feature the many windows and open spaces I'd imagined when I accepted a job at the epicenter of world power. I'd only watched "The West Wing" once, and my reality in Washington, DC was nothing like what that or any other Hollywood television series portrayed. At all.

The office to which I was assigned was just off the hallway belonging to the Situation Room and White House Mess dining room. The West Wing ground floor is not sexy, but it is one floor below the most powerful office in the world—the Oval Office—where every US president since 1909 has grappled with complex decisions that have shaped history.

In those early days, I learned just how much of the White House's mystique is built on contrasts—history layered upon routine, gravity intermingled with the mundane. Those halls may have echoed with the footsteps of giants, but on most mornings, they also rang with the familiar sounds of any other ordinary place of business, like mail carts rolling along carpeted floors and the footsteps of employees trying to get to their desk on time. The realities of service in that storied building were far less glamorous than I'd pictured, but the weight of responsibility felt as heavy as those claustrophobic ceilings.

The setting may not have been what I imagined, but nevertheless, at twenty-six years old, I was beyond thrilled and humbly honored to be working so close to the leader of the free world. It wasn't a glamorous setup—I shared an office with two other people, Cathy Alex and our direct boss, Deputy Assistant to the President for Management and Administration, Hector Irastorza—but for a girl from a small, but wonderful town, Kittanning, Pennsylvania, it was a dream come true.

My parents had always told me to keep my feet on the ground and my head held high, but nothing prepares you for the moment you realize you are a witness—sometimes even a participant—to events that will ripple outward and globally for generations. It's a strange thing to sit in a drab office, sip burnt coffee from a paper cup, and know that just a floor above, world leaders are pondering matters that could change history.

Outside of the ticking wall clock, it was quiet that Tuesday morning, but the mood would soon change in a way no one could have imagined.

I looked at my day planner. The date read September 11, 2001. President Bush wasn't in DC that day—he was in a second-grade classroom at Emma E. Booker Elementary School in Sarasota, Florida, reading to children. But his father, former president George H.W. Bush, was, and he stopped by my office to say hello to Hector, who used to work for him when he was President. I still remember the way the former president's presence could fill the room—his voice warm with Texan cadence yet edged with a gravitas earned over decades of service.

Conversations in the White House were often a curious mixture of the mundane and the momentous. For a fleeting moment, the day felt almost ordinary, the air filled with laughter and the gentle hum of camaraderie.

My chat with former President Bush was abruptly interrupted when the Secret Service hurried in and swept him out of the office. One second, he was there, and the next, he was gone. The suddenness of that moment—its abrupt, almost cinematic quality—left me blinking, unsure if I'd imagined it. At that point, we all knew a plane had hit the North Tower of World Trade Center in New York City, but we all still thought it was an accident.

My phone rang. It was my dear friend, Holly Kinser. She was watching her television in Philadelphia. The television is always on when you work in politics, and when I turned my head to the television on the credenza, I watched the second plane hit the South Tower in real time.

No one really understood the depth of what was unfolding, including the news anchors. Initially, people thought a small plane had mistakenly veered into the WTC's North Tower at 8:46 AM, but at 9:03 AM, when the second plane hit the South Tower live on television, it was clear this was no accident.

America was under attack.

At that moment, I was asked to run up to the second floor to help evacuate Vice President Dick Cheney's staff. As I started moving, Secret Service agents rushed him past me and my office to the bunker below the White House. Other agents told the women to remove their high heels and run for their lives. A third plane had just slammed into the Pentagon only three miles away from the White House, and United Flight 93 had crashed in a field outside of Shanksville, Pennsylvania a short time after that.

The normally rigid order of the West Wing had given way to chaos. Outside, sirens wailed, and helicopters thundered overhead as the Secret Service secured the building. Phones barely rang, the systems were overloaded and shutting down, delivering fragments of information—some true, some rumor, all alarming.

There were eight members of the political staff left in the building, including me: I'd been helping others to evacuate while thinking the unimaginable. Someone had obviously wanted to harm the United States, but the culprit was unclear. I knew Afghanistan was a volatile country with a dangerous leadership running it, but the words "Taliban" or "Al-Qaeda" had never crossed my lips.

The Secret Service told me in no uncertain terms that I should get out of the building. Hector looked at me and said I could stay if I wanted, but, also uncertain of the situation, he couldn't guarantee my safety.

I needed to decide whether to stay or go. I grabbed my purse and my bag, began throwing everything on my desk into them, then started toward the West Wing basement door. But I'd no sooner passed through the threshold when I stopped in my tracks.

No, I would not leave.

I turned around on my high heels that day and went back inside, not knowing what to expect.

And that was my first major pivot.

When I replay that pivotal day in my mind, the details still feel vivid and raw, as if etched into my bones. In my memories, the corridors of the White House—normally filled with a palpable sense of purpose and tradition—now pulsed with an unfamiliar urgency.

In the office, it was surreal, but for those of us who stayed, there was a job to do. The vice president was busy working with the secretary of transportation, Norm Mineta, and the rest of us were diligently accounting for all fourteen cabinet secretaries, approximately 4,500 planes in the air over the US that were being grounded to the nearest airport by the FAA, and, most importantly, the safety of the president and first lady.

Even amid a crisis, the machinery of government had to turn, and we became its gears, improvising as procedures did not keep up with the moment's spiraling demands. There was an unspoken pact among us: We would hold steady for as long as it took.

We watched the Twin Towers collapse and disintegrate into mangled heaps of concrete, steel, and glass. Manhattan resembled a dystopian wasteland. Still, I knew I couldn't leave the White House—something compelled me to stay. Was it divine, or was it sheer will? I didn't know.

Facing Your Fork in the Road

I didn't know it at the time, but I had arrived at my fork in the road. Looking back on it now, I recognize this as a make-or-break moment. My split-second decision took me to the next level and has since enabled me to rise even higher.

Of course, in that moment, I didn't have a term for it; there was no "Power Pivot" model I could consciously turn to. But this was a defining instance in my life. How could I have known that making the choice to stay meant I would end up as the first-ever employee of the newly formed White House Office for Homeland Security?

I couldn't.

But I did.

It had been quite the journey to the White House, made up of a continual series of small pivots. It began with family. My uncle, Doyle Corman, was a state senator in Pennsylvania. My cousin, Jake Corman, also became a Pennsylvania state senator. I followed in their footsteps and interned for Pennsylvania Governor Tom Ridge, who would later become Director then Secretary of Homeland Security. That opportunity happened because I met someone at a wedding who helped connect me with my first internship.

I moved to Harrisburg, Pennsylvania, lived in an extra bedroom belonging to a then-stranger, and interned in the governor's office during the summer of 1996, before my senior year of college. I ended up leaving college a semester early because I was offered, and accepted, a full-time position in the governor's office that paid $18,000 a year. Then one thing led to another.

Small pivots.

But if you look closer, none of these steps existed in isolation. Each decision, each fork—no matter how minor it seemed at the time—created a chain reaction that propelled me closer to those critical junctures. Accepting an underpaid government job meant trading comfort for possibility, and that willingness to step into the unknown became my compass. It wasn't always glamorous, and certainly not always obvious, but those leaps of faith—made quietly, humbly—built the foundation for every defining opportunity that followed.

Had I chosen to leave the West Wing basement, who knows where I would have ended up that day—or in life—but it certainly wouldn't have been the Situation Room.

That's a perfect summary, though maybe dramatic, for a pivot mindset—knowing when to change course and how to adapt. If you're working within an organization or company, it's the difference between staying ahead or falling behind. In those high-stakes moments, adaptation isn't just survival—it's the seed of progress.

That is the essence of a pivot: not just the grand gestures, but the courage to adapt, to commit, and to trust that the smallest step can lead to the most extraordinary destination. And by the time I stood in the Situation Room, history convulsing around us, I finally saw how every one of those steps had prepared me for this moment—not because I was fearless, but because I had learned, repeatedly, to say yes to the unknown.

Small pivots, repeated with intention, become the building blocks of our lives.

CHAPTER 1

THE VALUE OF SMALL PIVOTS

After that summer internship in Harrisburg, I returned to college to finish my final year of school feeling changed, and a little older. I'd just experienced "real life," and it was a fabulous feeling.

The world outside the lecture halls and dorm rooms had left its mark on me—subtle, but transformative. I noticed it in how I thought about my future, how I approached challenges, and how I began to see even the smallest decisions as opportunities rather than obstacles.

Just as the fall semester was winding down, I got a call from Governor Ridge's office, and they offered me a full-time position in his public liaison office in the Capitol.

I still remember the call. It was one of those moments in my life where time slowed and possibilities branched in my mind in all directions. Of course, I accepted the job. So, I left school. I had just one class to complete. My Westminster College professor, understanding the unique chance I'd been offered, allowed me to write a paper instead of attending class.

Moving to Harrisburg permanently was another leap into the unknown. I packed my things, nerves and excitement tangled together, and set out for the state capital, a place I barely knew. There, over the next four years, I immersed myself in the world of politics and public service, working for both the governor and a state lobbying firm. The city became my classroom, its fast pace and high stakes my curriculum.

At the age of twenty-five, I joined the Bush presidential campaign trail—a journey for me that would have seemed utterly improbable just a few years earlier. Although I did not know it then, my experience working on that campaign started with a pivot: leaving the comforts of Harrisburg, Pennsylvania, for a Presidential Campaign.

The campaign was relentless, a blur of long hours, fast-food meals, and adrenaline-fueled uncertainty. On the campaign trail, I traveled to many parts of the country, each one new to me. My work ranged from advance operations to grassroots political outreach on the ground, including meeting with local officials and knocking on doors. It was demanding work. It was *grunt* work—phone banks, driving long distances, putting up yard signs, fetching coffee—but we were all part of something larger: electing a president.

The campaign trail is its own education. You learn to adapt quickly, to anticipate needs before they arise, and to function on little sleep. The camaraderie that forms in the trenches is unlike any other; you find yourself bonding with colleagues through shared exhaustion, laughter, and the unspoken understanding that you are all in it together, each playing a small, but vital part in a greater mission.

The grunt work became even more demanding, if that were possible. First at the Republican National Convention in Philadelphia, then during the infamous Florida recount, and eventually with President-elect George W. Bush's transition team. The stakes grew higher and the tasks more consequential. All that hard work, small and big decisions along the way, and some luck, is how I ended up working in the White House basement.

Just weeks after 9/11, the terror campaign against America continued with the worst biological attack in American history. Anonymous letters laced with anthrax started showing up in the mailrooms of media organizations like NBC News and the *New York Post* in New York City, and in congressional offices, including those of Senator Patrick Leahy and Senator Tom Daschle, in Washington, DC.

This unleashed a nationwide panic, disrupted mail service and government operations for months, and sent the sales of the antibiotic used to treat anthrax, ciprofloxacin, soaring. The bio attack killed five people, including photojournalist Bob Stevens of American Media, the publisher of the *National Enquirer,* and it sickened seventeen others.

On October 8, 2001—the same day the anthrax was discovered at the national media outlets headquartered in New York City—President Bush announced to a joint session of Congress an executive order establishing the White House Office of Homeland Security, which would become my new assignment. He appointed my old boss from Pennsylvania, then–Governor Tom Ridge, to run it.

Since I was already working in the White House, I was considered employee number one of the new White House Office of Homeland Security, which later became the Homeland Security Council, and Governor Ridge was employee number two. The two of us, five others from Pennsylvania—Mark Holman, Carl Buchholz, Barbara Chafee, Duncan Campbell, and Bob Giles, who had married my mom weeks before—and Admiral Charles S. Abbot, a four-star admiral with a distinguished career in homeland security, became the original eight of the office.

We worked fifteen-hour days, seven days a week with one unified mission: Keep America safe.

When we began, life was chaotic. My days in the office began at 6:00 AM, with CIA briefings at 6:30 AM, followed by Governor Ridge briefing the president at 7:10 AM. This was before remote work, just the beginning of BlackBerrys, and years from smartphones, so we were in the office constantly, late at night and, of course, on the weekends.

Governor Ridge had moved to DC from Harrisburg, but his family had stayed there so his children, Lesley and Tommy, could finish the school year and transition out of the governor's mansion. As a Vietnam veteran and a dedicated public servant, he was stepping into a new chapter of national service after the horrific attacks of 9/11.

There was an atmosphere of urgency, pressure, and shared purpose. Every day brought fresh dangers, new intelligence to decipher, and new challenges to overcome. The anthrax attacks, the declaration of war against Afghanistan, and reports of terrorist plots across the globe compounded the sense of crisis. There were moments when the responsibilities before us seemed overwhelming, especially when news broke of a fresh threat, another letter, or another heartbreak for families somewhere across the country.

Despite the unrelenting pace, the days stretched endlessly, and the nights offered little reprieve, we found strength in our mission and in each other, forging ahead with determination and resolve. Our team was bound together by a shared purpose: ensuring that what happened on 9/11 would never happen again.

President Bush and Vice President Cheney wanted Governor Ridge nearby, so he and I had small, windowless offices in the West Wing. He had his own and I shared mine with three other colleagues. Our offices were located between the vice president's office and the Roosevelt Room, steps from the Oval Office.

Being this close to power was both a rush and brought immense pressure. We were actively shaping how the nation responded to one of the most significant crises in United States history. There was no roadmap for what we were doing; every protocol, every policy was being written in real time, often in response to events that arrived with little warning and no precedent.

Looking back, I now see how I didn't really grasp the magnitude of the historic events unfolding around me. Those significant moments didn't register until I was much older. At the time, I was in my late twenties and exhausted, as everyone else was. It was the weight of the responsibility that kept propelling us forward.

We focused on securing our country, building an infrastructure to enable state and local officials to communicate effectively—something that failed on 9/11—and ensuring that intelligence agencies coordinated to disrupt plots before they could materialize. We were a new team, building the foundation of Homeland Security from the ground up.

Helping build the White House Office of Homeland Security in its infancy was among the most profound honors of my life. We grew to 120 people strong and figuring it out as we went along.

Our efforts led Congress to create the Department of Homeland Security, which combined 260,000 employees and twenty-two agencies under one roof with the purpose of helping better coordinate our national security. It was the first new federal agency since the Department of Veterans Affairs was established by Congress in 1989.

As the department took shape and its future stretched out before it, I realized this was the right moment for me to move on.

I had given my all in service to President George W. Bush and Governor Ridge, but I needed new and different challenges to grow professionally. When Governor Ridge became the first Secretary of Homeland Security, I chose not to join him at the department. Instead, I went to work for his best friend, David Girard DiCarlo, at the law firm Blank Rome. Although I had the choice to take a different role at the new department, it was time to broaden my experience and reach the next level in my career.

Each of these choices—none of them easy, all of them pivotal—weren't made with perfect foresight. They were, however, made with a willingness to step into the unknown, to embrace uncertainty as a catalyst for growth. Each small pivot, when I dared to take it, opened doors I had never even realized were in front of me.

So, you see, when I changed course in the threshold of the West Wing basement door on 9/11, it changed my life. You can't make a change if you don't take a chance. And that's what I did.

Think about how all of this came about. How a few small decisions set the stage for the rest of my life. Had I not left home that summer and taken that first internship, would I be where I am now. Would I have discovered that I really like the inner workings of government, or learned the subtle art of influence, persuasion, and service?

Looking back now, I see my life not as a series of grand, orchestrated moves, but as a collection of small pivots. Each one nudged me in a new direction, sometimes gently, sometimes with force, but always with purpose. In the end, it is these small pivots—the risks we take, the challenges we embrace, the chances we seize—that shape not just our careers, but our very selves.

CHAPTER 2

EMBRACING THE PROCESS

Embracing the process means accepting that change is seldom linear, and progress rarely unfolds according to our imagined script. It really is a process, and going back to September 11, 2001, choosing to stay in the White House instead of evacuating was an immediate pivot I made. In the space of a few breathless seconds, the course of my life was altered by a lightning-fast decision I made in the face of crisis.

Not all choices, of course, demand such rapid response. Some major shifts in my life have unfolded slowly, over years of quiet consideration, or through the gentle accumulation of smaller choices that eventually revealed themselves as turning points. At times, the window for change was wide open; at others, it slammed shut in an instant, forcing my hand.

But here's the truth that has revealed itself over and over: every action, every risk, every triumph and setback in my life up to that date had unknowingly prepared me for the moment I had to decide. That decision on 9/11—one that transformed the arc of my personal and professional life—did not come from nowhere. It was the echo of hundreds of smaller decisions, made day after day, often without drama or recognition.

This is not about self-congratulation or self-promotion—it is a call to self-awareness. Open your eyes. Pay attention to the story you're writing with your everyday actions, even when it seems mundane. Look up, put one foot in front of you, and make *your* pivot.

The notion of "the pivot" isn't reserved only for moments of high drama or obvious crisis. It's about the ongoing willingness to see the truth of your circumstances, to challenge your assumptions, and to take intentional action repeatedly.

This is not a self-help book—not in the traditional sense, anyway. It is more about self-drive, about the force within you that refuses to settle for inertia. No one else is going to do the work for you; you must do it yourself. We have all heard this time and again. The uncomfortable truth is that while others may encourage or advise, at the end of the day, you're the one responsible for moving toward your own transformation. Putting a plan in place, even if it changes one hundred times, is about acting with intention. The plan itself is not always the end goal—it's the willingness to plan, to adjust, and to risk vulnerability and imperfection that builds momentum and creates clarity as you go. That's what matters, and that's how you get to the next level. Not me, not your best friend, not your closest colleague, not your spouse, but *you*. That's the difference. And I'm more than happy to hand you a few navigational tools for your journey.

I never set out to write a book or travel the country talking about the Power Pivot. If you had asked me years ago, I might have laughed at the suggestion and been embarrassed. But as I've said repeatedly, conditions are constantly changing, and we must know how and when to adapt—which is, I guess, what I'm doing now. I'm living another pivot in real time and adapting my sense of purpose and direction to meet new needs—both my own, and those of others who find themselves at a crossroads.

Ideas Often Appear in the Unlikeliest Moments

There's a myth that inspiration descends in cinematic flashes, but ideas often arrive when we're least prepared—between obligations, in moments of boredom, or while our bodies go through familiar motions. Here's how all of this came about for me.

During the COVID-19 pandemic, like so many others, I struggled with boredom and frustration. The world had slowed to a crawl and, with it, the relentless forward motion of my own plans. On what was otherwise a mundane day, SoulCycle, which had been closed like every other fitness center in Washington, DC, had reopened in a parking lot on Capitol Hill.

My mind has always wandered when I exercise, and it is often when I do my most serious thinking. Though an instructor was yelling a mix of motivational platitudes, challenges, and mildly abusive encouragement in my ears, my mind was moving faster than my legs. In those moments—sweating, lungs burning, legs pumping—I found myself reflecting not just on where I was, but how I had gotten there.

I'm often asked how I have accomplished certain things both personally or professionally, but everything I've done and every time I've taken a chance or pivoted, I've done it very intentionally. I realized how powerful intention is—how every significant moment of change stems from an act of deliberate choice, not an accident. Even with all the negatives of COVID-19, many positive changes happened to people as well. All of us received the gift of time and reflection. People started sharing their successes and thoughts with each other. I was asked many times what I did when I wanted to make a change or take a risk. The more I reflected, the clearer it became that there is a hunger for honest accounts of transformation.

And so, I decided that day, sweating in a Capitol Hill parking lot, to start writing a blog and talk about my own "She did what!?" moments and to also highlight the moments of others as well. I wanted to share how I and other amazing women (and a few men) made their own pivots. I wanted to pull back the curtain on the process, to show that transformation is possible not because someone is extraordinary, but because they are willing to act with extraordinary intention.

I started by putting in writing clarity around the moments in my life when I anticipated making a change and my thought process around it, documenting what steps I took to get from where I was to where I wanted to be. I then started sharing my own and other "She did what?!" stories on LinkedIn.

What began as a blog during the pandemic evolved into an hour-long keynote on what became the "Power Pivot." It's a framework designed to help you move from feeling stuck, unmotivated, or frustrated, to becoming focused, energized, and equipped—not just with talk or self-reflection, but with tangible tools to take real steps toward meaningful change and reach the next level in your life.

Over time, I realized that the Power Pivot isn't limited to your professional life. The same principles apply when you're staring down a personal crossroads—when you're faced with loss, with opportunity, with the quiet discomfort of knowing that things can't stay the way they are. Perhaps you've reached a point in your personal life where you're done *hoping* to make a change and are ready to take concrete steps, but you aren't sure what they are or where to start. The Power Pivot applies here, too. You can't be stuck in a mindset of having done everything in your life one particular way. If you are, you will never get off the hamster wheel.

That's the whole point of a pivot; you're trying to break that mindset and the paradigm of your own life or situation. Transformation is not a one-time event; it's a discipline, a mindset, a willingness to risk being hopeful and to believe that "different" can be better. It means making conscious, deliberate decisions and thinking differently. This applies to women, and it applies to men. It applies to young adults and older adults.

When I started public speaking, I'd get frustrated when speakers' bureaus, corporations, policy-focused organizations, and others in the United States or even internationally would shoehorn me into one area, thinking that I only spoke to women's groups or that my message was only for women. Today, I have found that more men than women identify with making a strategic change or taking a risk and putting a plan in place to execute it. But that's not because women aren't doing it and men are—it's because we haven't always framed change as something either women or men are empowered to own. The stories we tell ourselves—and each other—shape our willingness to act. When we see ourselves as agents of change, as the authors and architects of our own lives, we claim the right to pivot.

Regardless of who you are, the difference between staying stagnant and making a true pivot often comes down to one thing: intention. Whether the change is small or seemingly seismic, choosing to act *deliberately* is what sets transformation in motion. The pivot isn't always dramatic; sometimes, it's the quiet shift, the decision to try again, to reimagine what's possible, or to move forward despite fear or fatigue.

To make all of it work takes the power of intention—intentional planning and intentional purpose that leads to intentional change. Over the past few years, I've identified three different distinct forms of Power Pivots: the Personal Pivot, the Business Pivot, and the Leadership Pivot. Each demands a different kind of clarity, courage, and execution, and each has the potential to redefine your trajectory.

The Personal Pivot asks you to confront your habits and your stories, to rewrite patterns that no longer serve you.

The Business Pivot challenges organizations, teams, and leaders to rethink strategy and adapt to new realities.

The Leadership Pivot, perhaps the most complex of all, requires stepping into uncertainty and guiding others through transformation—modeling resilience, vision, and accountability.

The pages that follow are a framework for strategic transformation, empowering you with the tools, insight, and conviction to take intelligent and calculated risks so you can execute your own Power Pivot. This is not about quick wins; it's about positioning yourself individually, as a leader or in business, for lasting, sustainable success. The Power Pivot Framework is here not only to inspire, but to provide a practical roadmap—a way to move from awareness to action, and from action to achievement. Because in the end, the process is ongoing, the learning is constant, and the next pivot is always within reach.

CHAPTER 3

IN THE BEGINNING

To truly appreciate the power of the pivot, of transformative change, we need to appreciate where we are in the present, where we are going, and where we are from. You can't chart a course toward the future if you don't truly consider the path you've traveled to get to the now.

In my case, as I've mentioned, I was born in Kittanning, Pennsylvania, in 1975. What an apropos year. 1975 was a banner year for pivots. With the end of the Vietnam War in April, the United States brought home its men and women in the military, and South Vietnam reunified with the North under a communist government. Ironically, that year, the United States and the communist Soviet Union conducted the Apollo-Soyuz Test Project, the first joint space mission, the beginning of a détente between the most powerful Cold War adversaries.

That spring, the world collectively held its breath. The images of helicopters evacuating the last Americans from Saigon, the uncertain faces of families beginning anew, the televised testimonies that recounted the cost of conflict—these were not simply headlines, but echoes in the lives of millions.

Even in small-town Pennsylvania, the reverberations of global decisions reached every family, every classroom, and every living room with a flickering TV. I was born into a world poised between relief at war's end and anxiety about what peace—and change—would bring.

In the United States, we saw a political pivot as the country began to recover from the Watergate scandal and the resignation of President Richard Nixon in 1974. Now, President Gerald Ford pivoted from the aftermath of the Watergate scandal to economic recovery as Americans slogged through crushing inflation, high unemployment, and a recession.

Economic shifts almost always force change, collectively and individually, to either survive or to thrive. The 1970s demanded reinvention—fuel shortages, jobs in flux, and societal roles shifting, especially for women and minorities.

The US Congress passed the Equal Credit Opportunity Act in 1974, which banned discrimination in lending based on gender or marital status, allowed more women to pivot from the home into professional opportunities outside the home. The timing was perfect, as 1975 was also deemed the International Women's Year by the United Nations, which galvanized the women's rights movement. Suddenly the landscape was different; doors previously shut to half the population creaked open, and the definition of possibility expanded. This was not only legislative change, but a seismic adjustment in the rhythm and expectations of daily life.

Change was happening everywhere in 1975; it ushered in the era of personal computing with the release of the Altair 8800, the first commercially successful personal computer. Bill Gates and

Paul Allen founded Microsoft in 1975 to develop software for it. So, 1975 was a year of life-changing endings, like the Vietnam War, and life-changing beginnings, like the personal computing era, with cultural milestones that continue to resonate.

Small Town Values

As a society, America—and the world—was pivoting in 1975, so it's fitting that's the year I was born. Kittanning is a beautiful town about forty-five minutes northwest of Pittsburgh, Pennsylvania. It sits on the Allegheny River and embodies quintessential America. It was an amazing place to grow up; quaint, idyllic, and pretty perfect. We were a close-knit community where everyone knew everyone. There were only 140 students in my Kittanning High School graduating class. Attending Kittanning High School was what you'd imagine it to be—football games, parties in the woods (yes, Mom, I was at them all), and summers spent on the river.

My upbringing was about as normal as it gets. I had lots of love from four grandparents, best friends, my brother, Jason (who I, of course, annoyed to death all day every day), and two fabulous parents, Kathy Giles and Denny Davis, both of whom were also born and raised in Kittanning.

Life was predictable, wholesome, and good. My family was lucky to have a stay-at-home mom for our early years. She was active and supportive in everything we did. My dad owned a small business—the car dealerships my grandfather started in 1957. My dad and my Papa Davis have always been the reason I enjoyed business. I would go to work often with my dad, and he still gives me sound advice and direction when I am making big and little decisions.

Here's how fortunate our family was: From when I was a baby until fourth grade, we lived next door to one set of my grandparents. When I was twelve years old, my family moved to downtown Kittanning, just a few blocks from my other set of grandparents. I was always surrounded by family and friends—good friends. In fact, my two best friends then, Samantha Starr and Kara Panchik, are still my two best friends to this day. They are now more sisters than friends.

I loved growing up how I did, it meant inheriting a certain worldview—a sense of belonging, continuity, and sometimes, limitation. There was a rhythm to the days, a predictability to the seasons, and a collective understanding that everyone's actions, for better or worse, rippled through the community. Neighbors didn't just lend a cup of sugar; they lent time, advice, and support through every chapter of life. In Kittanning, we celebrated victories together—like winning a Friday night football game or a local business thriving—and we faced tragedies as one.

When I was in high school and began looking for a college, I never even dreamed of or considered applying to Ivy League schools. I only applied to two schools and decided on Westminster College in Western Pennsylvania. It's a small liberal arts school with 1,200 students and could not have had a better college experience. I took advantage of all it had to offer. I received a fantastic education and made lifelong friends. I've stayed involved with the school to this day and sat on its board of directors for thirteen years.

It was at Westminster that I began to see the world beyond the forests and rivers of my hometown. My professors encouraged curiosity and debate, my fellow students brought fresh perspectives, and for the first time, I learned how to pivot—academically, socially, and personally. I learned that change, while daunting, could also be exhilarating. Westminster was the perfect size college for me, one that allowed for growth while allowing me to stay rooted in the familiar.

Pivoting into a Career

As I've mentioned, after completing my junior year, I spent a summer interning for then Governor Tom Ridge, a step that truly put me on the path for what I do today. At the time, I didn't even realize I had an interest in politics, but moving to Harrisburg, the capital of Pennsylvania, sounded like fun.

After a brief full-time job with the Governor, I went to a firm where I learned the business I'm in now. I was just twenty-two years old, and Stan Rapp and Bill Greenlee, the firm's namesake and founder, took a chance on me and offered me a job at their lobbying firm, Greenlee Associates.

At the same time, my parents were going through a difficult divorce. They had been married for twenty-seven years, never argued, and lived a happy life together. I was just as blindsided as everyone else when it happened. I did my best to internalize it and tried to help my mom as she worked through a painful, life-changing event. Stan and Bill were incredibly supportive and gave me the solid foundation I needed.

What they didn't know when they hired me, however, was that at the time, I knew nothing about lobbying. In fact, I had looked up the word "lobbyist" in the dictionary to try and understand what it was about and the work it entailed. I had no idea what a lobbyist or a lobbying firm did. It didn't really matter, because initially my role involved answering phones, making coffee, and paging people. Yes, paging. Remember those days?

It was all an invaluable experience, and I went on to spend almost four years at Greenlee Associates. Stan and Bill where instrumental in shaping me into who I am today. They, and the entire Greenlee team, became like family.

Looking back, those early days were both intimidating and formative. I learned to listen more than I spoke, to observe the subtle ways influence flowed through a room, and to recognize how preparation and persistence could open doors. Lobbying, I soon discovered, was less about power than about relationships and trust—a truth that would guide me through every future career pivot.

George W. Bush and My First Real Pivot

I know I've said the moment in the White House basement on 9/11 was my first Power Pivot, but when I look back, my first true pivot was when I tried to figure out how to get on the George W. Bush campaign for president in 1999.

Sure, I was already working in a fulfilling job that I loved, but working on a presidential campaign and working at the national level were the shiny objects I just had to have. So, I began laying the groundwork for how to get on the campaign.

I leaned into the power of networking, which was a skill I learned while at Greenlee Associates. I loved working to perfect it.

The list of people I knew who knew someone in Governor Bush's orbit was short, but it was strong. Governor Ridge was both close with former President George H.W. Bush and Governor Bush himself. At the time, I was dating my now husband, Joel Frushone, who was working for the Stevens & Schriefer Group, a media consulting firm that was both Governor Ridge's media consultant and part of Governor Bush's presidential media consulting team. So, I began with Stuart Stevens and Russ Schreifer

Making the most of my network enabled me to map out my plan to get a job on the campaign. I also found out who the key campaign people were, both at the higher levels and the grassroots workers.

Through my network connections and cold calling, I reached out to and spoke with anyone and everyone who would listen. This led me to fly to Austin, Texas, where the Bush for President campaign was headquartered. I had never been to Texas before, but I was ready to go because I had a plan. Still, making the decision to leave behind a great job and colleagues, a boyfriend, and close friends was not easy.

When I landed at the relatively new Austin-Bergstrom International Airport, I was determined to volunteer or to hopefully be hired on as staff. It didn't take long before I'd met several campaign staff who listened to this young, very eager woman and gave me an opportunity.

My first experience on a presidential campaign, was knocking on doors in New Hampshire. I never expected that I would start by briefing Governor Bush on national economic or agriculture policy; that wasn't part of my plan. My plan was to learn about as many aspects as possible of a presidential campaign. New Hampshire was the ideal training ground to get a comprehensive education on the campaign business.

Volunteering on the campaign in New Hampshire immersed me in the fast-paced, high-stakes environment of an early primary state. That first trip was more than just a political experience—it was pivotal. The relationships I built, knowledge I gained, and momentum we created opened new doors for me to work in other states—which included Virginia, Delaware, Pennsylvania and South Carolina—during the primary season. Each new state was a unique experience with new people, new challenges, and new lessons. The energy you carry in your early twenties combined with the intensity of a presidential campaign did more than just help me push through the exhaustion—it fueled me. The entire experience broadened my perspective, deepened my commitment, and sharpened my sense of purpose in ways that still shape how I lead today.

George W. Bush's primary victory over Senator John McCain of Arizona, a formidable opponent, who I had always admired and respected, secured him the Republican nomination. It brought us all back to Pennsylvania for the Republican National Convention in Philadelphia in August of 2000. That led to the Florida ballot recount later in 2000, and eventually to the transition team before now–President-elect Bush took his oath of office on January 20, 2001.

My first day in the White House was day one of the George W. Bush presidency. I was hired as the Deputy Director of Management and Administration, which is how I ended up with an office in the West Wing basement on that fateful September day in 2001.

I spent the first nine months in the role, which was truly about the "care and feeding" of the White House and the staff. The office oversaw the White House Military Office, which manages the operations of the White House compound, as well as all White House administration functions, and the management of political appointees.

Those first nine months were chaotic. We had to set up everyone's offices, decide access to the West Wing and the Executive Office of the President building, and navigate the highly political nature of these decisions. Everyone, of course, felt they deserved

West Wing access. Hector Irastorza, Cathy Alix, and I aimed to ensure that everything was decided and set up by August, so when senior staff returned from summer at the Western White House in Crawford, Texas in September, they could hit the ground running. Little did we know what was to come.

The events of September 11, 2001, changed everything. In an instant, uncertainty, fear, and responsibility collided. The country pivoted, and so did I. My role transformed overnight from logistics and administration to crisis management and support of national security. I learned to adapt under pressure, to lead with steadiness in chaos, and to anchor empathy in action. That day became a dividing line—not just for the nation, but for the direction of my own life.

Pivoting to the Private Sector and Back to School

After helping create the Department of Homeland Security, I pivoted from public service and left the White House to join the government affairs practice at Blank Rome, a national law firm. I stepped into the private sector with a clear goal: to broaden my experience.

I worked to grow the government affairs practice and eventually became the managing principal of Blank Rome Government Relations and served on the firm's executive committee. In that role, I built and managed strategic alliances with more than twenty international public affairs firms, expanding our global reach, and deepening our influence across borders.

While at Blank Rome I made another bold choice: to return to school at the age of forty to pursue an international master's in business administration. One of my goals of getting an MBA was to help me sit on corporate boards. This was an informed decision. I'd been told dozens of times that I couldn't be on a corporate board without at least some sort of finance profit-and-loss experience. Prior to returning to school, I had thought my expertise in government, policy, and regulation would open the doors. It didn't. I ran repeatedly into the same brick wall: my lack of finance experience.

So, I began putting a plan in place to go back to school—another intentional pivot. I looked for a business program where I could attend school while being a mom, a wife, and working full time. I found exactly what I needed at the McDonough School of Business at Georgetown University, a wonderful program designed for people with fifteen years or more of working experience. I enrolled, and it turned out to be one of the most rewarding times of my life.

The two years of studying, traveling, learning, preparing, and planning to get on a corporate board went by incredibly fast. Pursing an MBA also helped me develop the business skills I didn't have and would need to start my own government affairs firm.

The program was module driven, which meant I'd live in a foreign country for an intense period studying, and in between, be at home living my normal life as a mom, wife, and managing partner. My son, Oliver, was six years old, and my husband, Joel, was spending an exceptional amount of time in Africa for work, making the logistics tough to handle. My mom was instrumental during this time and made sure Oliver did not miss anything.

The program took me to Brazil twice, Spain, China, UAE, and, of course, Washington DC. When the module commenced at Georgetown's main campus in DC, a mere two miles from my house, I had to live on campus instead of at home, and so did my classmates from across the globe. It pushed me hard and made me stronger, sharper, and more resilient businesswoman.

Again, it took me over two years to complete, but you simply cannot grow or move forward if you just wish for something like a corporate board position *and not actively do something about it!*

It's been said that a dream without a goal is a wish, and that much is true. I put in the extra effort into going back to school because I knew what my end goal was, which was getting the experience I could point to when pursuing opportunities. I didn't just wish for it. The program gave me three executive MBAs, one from Georgetown, one from ESADE Business and Law School in Barcelona, Spain, and one from Fundaçáo Getulio Vargas (FGV) in Rio de Janerio, Brazil, and a thesis on corporate inversions, which were hot at the time.

This is what I call an *intentional pivot*; I saw an end goal and then put a strategy in place to get there. The total effort took me three years—or more realistically, three and a half—before landing on my first corporate board. It was an exhausting, yet exhilarating experience, and I will never have a single regret for doing it. I'm so happy I did.

If there's a thread connecting all these stories, it's that each pivot was shaped by my roots as much as my ambitions. Small town values provided a foundation of resilience and loyalty, while the larger historical tides influenced what was possible and necessary. At every turn, I have had to decide—often with uncertainty—whether to cling to the comfort of the familiar or to leap into the unknown.

This leads me to *your* intentional pivot.

Read on.

THE POWER PIVOT

PERSONAL

CHAPTER 4
BEING INTENTIONAL

"A very small shift in direction can lead to a very meaningful change in destination."

–James Clear[1]

The dictionary defines the word "intentional" as something "done by intention or design with purpose."[2] But what does that mean when it comes to living your life with intention? I want to begin by focusing on the deeply personal responsibility we all have in changing our lives—if, and only if, it is something you're genuinely ready to do.

No one else is going to make changes for you. Change is not a package that will arrive at your door courtesy of someone else's effort or concern. If you're unhappy, whether it's in your job, your marriage, or everyday life, you must be the architect of your own transformation. Recognizing and accepting this is

---

1 James Clear, *Atomic Habits: An Easy & Proven Way to Build Good Habits & Break Bad Ones* (Avery, 2018), Kindle.

2 By permission. *Merriam-Webster's Collegiate® Dictionary*, 11th ed. (2019), under "intentional."

both liberating and daunting. It requires honesty with yourself, the courage to admit when change is needed, and the resolve to see it through. If you're waiting for someone to swoop in and make things better, you may be waiting a lifetime. The truth is, you are the only one who can chart the course and put a plan in place to get where you want to go.

Be intentional.

That means making a conscious choice to direct your energy, focus, and time toward what matters most. For example, as I mentioned, when I decided to go back to college at forty years old, it wasn't a mere whim or a fleeting notion. I made a deliberate decision, born out of reflection and a yearning for growth. From the moment that idea took root, it took me about three and a half years of steady commitment before I found myself attending business school and, eventually, landing my corporate board seat. Sometimes, change can happen overnight, but more often, it unfolds like a long journey, requiring years of planning, sacrifice, and persistent effort. This is also where long-term vision becomes essential. It's the compass that keeps you oriented when progress feels slow and your destination becomes obscured for untold reasons.

You must be in control of your own destiny. For me, it starts when an idea or desire comes to mind. It's like a seed—you can feel it, sometimes faintly at first, quietly insisting that something needs to change. It could be a longing for more fulfillment at work, a desire to be healthier, or a yearning to create impact beyond yourself. That idea percolates—it sits in your mind and heart, nudging you, growing roots. It becomes persistent enough that you can't ignore it any longer.

When I feel that stirring within me, I don't wait for motivation to magically appear; I create and sustain it through daily rituals that keep me anchored in my purpose. I'm very structured about my mornings. Each day, I start by reading the news (I get five real newspapers delivered to my house: the *New York Times, Washington Post, New York Post, Wall Street Journal,* and *Financial Times*), I then read a chapter in a book on leadership or strategy and finish my hour by writing my goals for the day. This isn't just a habit—it's intentional nourishment for my mind, a way to ensure I'm moving toward whatever pivot I'm aiming to make. My mornings are sacred, a space carved out for growth and forward momentum.

Let's say I decide I want to become more productive and mentally happier. I would start with research: reading books, exploring articles, listening to podcasts—gathering knowledge from those who've traveled similar paths. I jot down the key takeaways, the habits and ideas that might help me get from where I am now to where I want to be. Then, the real work begins. I start implementing those changes, even if they're small at first.

If my goal is a specific Power Pivot in my work life, I begin by immersing myself in business books tailored to my goal and then assemble a strategy—a roadmap. For instance, I might declare, "In the next three months, I want to clearly define what I need to do to develop a deep understanding of US and European AI policy. This isn't just a hypothetical scenario—it's a real goal of mine at the moment. That's my first milestone. Next, I'll set a six-month plan, identifying three to five changes or additions to my life that will help me to meet that goal. Finally, I break down the journey into smaller, achievable steps, each with its own timeline. This structure transforms ambition into action, and action into achievement.

Planning the Intentional Pivot

Making an intentional pivot is not a one-time event. It is a process—a living, breathing evolution.

Sometimes, despite your best-laid plans, you may get halfway along the path you carefully mapped out, only to realize it isn't leading you exactly where you want to go. Circumstances changed, or you discovered a new passion or a different calling. Or you simply find that what you set out to do doesn't resonate as deeply as it once did. And that's okay. In fact, it's not only okay—it's normal. The good news is that the path is always flexible. You don't have to rigidly stick to a course that no longer serves you. Instead, make small, thoughtful adjustments to your current plan, course corrections that reflect your new insights and aspirations.

This agility will steer you back on course—or onto a new, even more fulfilling path—and still enable you to reach your true destination. And from that moment of honest recalibration, draw renewed strength and motivation knowing that recognizing the need for a shift or small pivot and boldly acting on it isn't a setback, but a sign of wisdom, growth, and a deepened commitment to living with intention.

What gives you the courage and the strength to do all of this is the intentional planning and the purposeful focus that guide you toward change. They are the rudders that move you forward, making meaningful change possible. If you put the right processes in place before making the change, it becomes far less intimidating. *Preparation breeds confidence.* If you are aiming to reach a specific accomplishment, what truly matters isn't luck or talent alone. It is the *hard* work, discipline, and dedication you invest in the process to reach your goal.

Being intentional, to me, means taking the time and effort to understand where you're going. It's about clarity—knowing not just what you want, but also why you want it, and how you plan to get there.

For example, if your goal is to earn a promotion at work or become a partner at your firm, ask yourself: *If I intentionally want to reach that next level, what are the concrete tactical steps within my control that I can take to make it happen?* How can you deliberately and consciously use each step to position yourself, get noticed by leadership, and put yourself squarely on the path to success?

The same principle applies to personal goals. If your aim is to get healthier, maybe that means committing to going to the gym four days a week or working with a nutritionist to build better habits. The key is to ask yourself, *What intentional planning will help me achieve the result I want?* For any pivot you hope to make, having a plan behind it gives you the courage to follow through and make real, lasting change. It turns intention into action and transforms dreams into reality.

CHAPTER 5

THE POWER PIVOT: THE FRAMEWORK FOR PERSONAL SUCCESS

The concept of the Power Pivot offers a powerful framework for personal transformation and achievement. It serves as a metaphor for making intentional, strategic shifts in your mindset, habits, and actions, all designed by you to unlock your full potential and achieve extraordinary success.

Think of it like sailing. You can't control the wind—life's external circumstances, unexpected setbacks, or the actions of others. But by intentionally adjusting your sails—altering your mindset, refining your habits, and taking deliberate action—you can change your course and still reach your destination. The journey may not be linear, but the direction is still yours to choose.

The Power Pivot: Unlocking Your Path to Personal Success

Now, you might be wondering, *What exactly is the difference between a "pivot" and a "Power Pivot?"* Imagine you're on a basketball court, one foot firmly planted while the other moves freely. This stance gives you the ability to shift direction, dodge obstacles, and seize opportunities with agility. In life, a Power Pivot is that intentional, grounded shift—rooted in your core values and strengths—that empowers you to change course, overcome barriers, and move toward your goals with clarity and confidence. The crucial difference is all about *intention*. It's about deciding, with conviction, that you're not just drifting with the current, but steering your life with purpose.

There are three key pillars of the Power Pivot that can propel you toward individual success:

1. Embracing a Growth Mindset
2. Building Disciplined Habits
3. Leveraging Your Unique Strengths

Pillar One: Embracing a Growth Mindset

The first pillar of the Power Pivot is adopting a growth mindset. This is the foundation of any meaningful change. A growth mindset, as pioneered by psychologist Carol Dweck, is the belief that your abilities, intelligence, and talents can be developed through effort, learning, and persistence. It's the opposite of a fixed mindset, which assumes your qualities are innate and unchangeable.

A growth mindset is not just a philosophy—it's a practical tool for progress. It means you see setbacks not as failures, but as valuable feedback. The key is that this mindset makes your goals achievable, even when they stretch your limits, mind, body, and soul. Being realistic is important, too. For example, if you want to Power Pivot to become a professional violinist, but have never picked up a violin, it may not be the best investment of your time and resources. On the other hand, if you want to move from working for someone else to starting your own business, a growth mindset is essential—it lets you recognize your potential while grounding your ambitions. I'll explain later how I navigated this when I started my own government affairs firm after working at a law firm for thirteen years.

A growth mindset is your first Power Pivot because it shifts how you view challenges. Instead of seeing obstacles as proof of your limitations, you see them as invitations to learn and grow. Several research studies from Stanford University confirm that individuals with a growth mindset are far more likely to embrace challenges, persist through setbacks, and achieve higher levels of success in academics, careers, and life.

So, how do you cultivate a growth mindset? Here are three practical steps:

- **Reframe Failure.** Instead of saying, "I failed," say, "I'm learning." Every setback is a lesson that brings you closer to your goal. If you applied for a job, you really wanted and didn't get it, ask for honest feedback, use it to improve, and position yourself to succeed when a similar opportunity arises.
- **Seek Feedback.** Actively ask for constructive criticism from mentors, colleagues, or friends. Think of it as your personal GPS for growth. For example, ask your supervisor or boss, "Could you share some feedback on why

I didn't receive that promotion? I'd also like to bounce some ideas off you to make sure I'm better prepared to become successful next time." Even uncomfortable feedback is a gift—it's information you can use to get better, faster, and stronger.

- **Celebrate Effort, Not Just Results.** Recognize and honor the hard work you put in—even if the outcome isn't perfect. This builds resilience and a positive mindset. Two of my biggest pet peeves are pouting or dwelling on a setback when something doesn't go your way. Instead, use the constructive feedback and what you learned as steppingstones to celebrate what you can do next.

When you embrace a growth mindset, you're planting your pivot foot in possibility. You're telling yourself, *I may not be there yet, but I can get there.* That is always the most important first step in unlocking your potential.

Pillar Two: Build Disciplined Habits

Success isn't made in a single grand moment of triumph; it's built, brick by brick, through the small, consistent actions you take every day. Your habits are the true building blocks of your future. To make a Power Pivot, you need to intentionally design habits that align with and drive you toward your goals.

Let's look at an example. James Clear, the renowned author of *Atomic Habits: An Easy & Proven Way to Build Good Habits & Break Bad Ones*, didn't become a bestselling writer overnight. Before fame, he struggled with the same inconsistency and procrastination that plagues us all. His Power Pivot was a commitment to writing just two pages a day, no matter what. That small, disciplined habit compounded over time, eventually growing into a blog with millions of readers and a book that has affected countless lives. Clear's story is a testament to the fact that success doesn't require Herculean effort—just consistent, intentional habits. One of my favorite takeaways from his book is this: "*A very small shift in direction can lead to a very meaningful change in destination.*"[3]

Caitlin Clark's rise to WNBA stardom is another example of how making an intentional Power Pivot through steady, consistent, and intentional habits can transform your trajectory. Her transition from college basketball to the professional league is daunting. To meet this new challenge, Clark made an intentional Power Pivot. She committed to an intense off-season routine—taking three hundred shots a day, including one hundred three-pointers, one hundred mid-range shots, and one hundred free throws, along with strength training four to five times a week.[4] Her focused investment into daily habits didn't produce overnight results, but over time, those habits compounded, equipping her to thrive at the next level. Clark's journey proves that meaningful change isn't about sudden leaps, but about intentionally designing and sustaining habits aligned with your goals.

Why are habits so powerful? Because they create momentum. According to various studies and authors, it takes an average of sixty-six days, sometimes as few as thirty, to form a new habit. Once ingrained, the action becomes automatic, liberating your mind for higher-level thinking and creativity. Habits are the engine of your Power Pivot—they keep you moving forward even when motivation fades.

---

3 James Clear, *Atomic Habits: An Easy & Proven Way to Build Good Habits & Break Bad Ones* (Avery, 2018), Kindle.

4 Talya Minsberg, "The Secret to Caitlin Clark's Shooting Power," *New York Times*, April 5, 2024.

Here's how to build disciplined habits for your own Power Pivot:

- **Start Small.** Choose one habit that directly aligns with your goal. Want to get fit? Start with just ten minutes of exercise daily. Aspire to advance your career? Dedicate fifteen minutes each day to expand your knowledge or networking.
- **Use Triggers.** Anchor your new habit to something you already do. For example, if you want to read more, commit to reading ten pages immediately after your morning coffee. This consistency builds association and makes it easier to stick with the habit.
- **Track Your Progress.** Use a journal or app to mark your daily wins. This creates a visual reminder of your commitment and helps build momentum. Even if you're skeptical about journaling, tracking small wins can boost motivation by making your progress tangible and real. I use a journal every morning to track my progress.

Let me share a personal anecdote. A few years ago, I wanted to improve my productiveness and mental health. What I found was a book that changed my life—*The 5AM Club: Own Your Morning. Elevate Your Life.* by Robin Sharam. There are so many lessons I learned and tactics I took from Robin. The one simple habit that changed everything was waking up at five o'clock every morning. That single pivot brought more structure to my days, gave me uninterrupted time to read and write, and, over time, fueled a stronger intention to propel myself forward both professionally and personally.

The ripple effect was profound: not only did my mornings change, but so did my evenings. Suddenly, the lure of staying up too late or having one more glass of wine faded, knowing my alarm would ring at 5:00 AM. And here's my little secret about the "5AM Club": I wake up at 5:03. That tiny shift helps me mentally conquer the challenge of rising early.

Disciplined habits, no matter how small, create exponential impact. By building them intentionally, you're not just making a pivot; you're putting in place a system that makes success inevitable.

Pillar Three: Leverage Your Unique Strengths

The third pillar of the Power Pivot is all about leveraging your unique strengths. Each of us has a one-of-a-kind blend of talents, experiences, and passions that make us extraordinary. A true Power Pivot isn't about emulating someone else's path to success—it's about amplifying what makes you, you.

How do you discover your strengths? One powerful tool to start with is self-reflection. Ask yourself: *What activities make me lose track of time? What do others often compliment me on?* You can also use assessments like StrengthsFinder or simply ask trusted friends and colleagues for their perspective. Remember Pillar One—*seek feedback*. Once you identify your strengths, the next step is to leverage and use them strategically. Lean into what you do best as you chart your Power Pivot.

Here are three ways to leverage your strengths:

- **Align Your Goals with Your Strengths.** If you're a natural communicator, pursue roles or projects that involve speaking, writing, or teaching. If you're analytical, seek out problem-solving or data-driven tasks where those strengths shine.

- **Build a Personal Brand.** Showcase your strengths through your work, on social media, and in your networking. Let the world see what makes you exceptional and what you stand for.
- **Collaborate with Others.** Your strengths complement those of the people around you. Build a network where you can exchange value—like a team of superheroes, each bringing unique powers to achieve something greater together.

Here's a real-world example from my own journey and how I accomplished one of these goals. Five years ago, I had no personal brand to speak of. No Instagram or Facebook presence, and just a few followers on three different LinkedIn accounts. That changed when Madeline Fetterly, a new acquaintance who was several years younger and much more knowledgeable about social media, approached me with an idea.

She pitched me on a plan: allow her to build an online brand for me—one I was comfortable with that felt authentic, highlighted my interests, and advanced the causes I support. We started slow, with Madeline managing my digital presence as her "side hustle." Over time, her dedication and vision blossomed into "Be the Brand," a successful agency specializing in personal branding. A sizable portion of our success came from her commitment to collaboration in helping clients like me highlight what made us unique. That experience taught me an invaluable lesson: when you leverage what makes you special and seek help from others who complement your strengths, you're not just making a pivot; you're positioning yourself to shine in a way only you can.

CHAPTER 6

HOW TO START THE POWER PIVOT

Now that we've explored the three pillars—Embracing a Growth Mindset, Building Disciplined Habits, and Leveraging Your Unique Strengths—how do you put them into action? Your Power Pivot is a personal journey, but here's a simple outline to help you get started:

- **Reflect and Assess.** Set aside ten minutes this week to write down your goals and pinpoint one area where you feel stuck. Schedule this time on your calendar or set a reminder in your phone right now. Ask yourself: *What's holding me back? Is it my mindset, my habits, or am I not fully using my strengths?*
- **Choose One Pivot.** Select one small shift to focus on. It could be reframing a recent setback, starting a new habit

like journaling for five minutes a day, or leaning into a strength by taking on a project that highlights it.

- **Create a Thirty-Day Challenge.** Commit to your chosen pivot for thirty days. Track your progress daily and celebrate every small win. Research shows a month is long enough to build momentum and start seeing real results.

Let's look at how this works in practice. Entrepreneur Jesse Itzler, in his bestselling book *Living with a SEAL: 31 Days Training with the Toughest Man on the Planet*, chronicles how thirty days can shock your system, build momentum, and prove what you're truly capable of. In 2010, after watching Navy SEAL David Goggins run a solo one-hundred-mile race, Itzler invited him to live with his family for a month—including his wife, Sara Blakely, the entrepreneur who founded Spanx—on the condition that he do everything Goggins commanded. The result? Those intense thirty days unlocked new levels of mental toughness and discipline, shaping Itzler's habits and mindset for years to come.

Let's make this even more practical. Imagine you want to pivot toward a healthier lifestyle. You could:

- **Adopt a growth mindset** by viewing exercise as an opportunity to grow stronger, not just a chore.
- **Build a habit** of walking fifteen minutes every day after lunch.
- **Leverage your strength of discipline** by creating a workout schedule—and sticking to it.

Or, if you're pivoting toward a career change:

- **Embrace a growth mindset** by learning a new skill, like coding, design, or public speaking.
- **Build a habit of dedicating** thirty minutes a day to studying, networking, or refining your resume.
- **Leverage your creative strengths** by building a portfolio that highlights your unique perspective and voice.

The beauty of the Power Pivot is its flexibility. It's a universal framework that adapts to any goal—personal, professional, or creative. At its heart, it's about seizing control of your direction and intentionally moving toward the life you want. Real transformation doesn't happen by accident; it happens through intentional choices, repeated over time.

Remember that success isn't about being perfect or having all the answers. *None of us are, and none of us do.* It's about having the courage to pivot—to shift your mindset, habits, and actions toward what truly lights you up and will propel you forward. The Power Pivot is your tool to break free from feeling stuck, to transform challenges into opportunities, and build a life filled with purpose and impact.

So, here's my challenge to you:

This week, take just one small step toward your Power Pivot. Reframe a limiting belief. Start a new habit. Celebrate a strength. You don't have to change everything overnight—just plant your pivot foot and begin moving in a new direction. That one step can spark momentum, and momentum can change your life. It did for me, and it can for you.

You have the power to pivot. The path is yours to create, so step forward boldly, own your journey, and make it happen for you.

THE POWER PIVOT

BUSINESS

CHAPTER 7

THE POWER PIVOT FOR BUSINESS

As we've seen time and again, the most successful businesses pivot when their current model stops working, but when the CEOs, founders, or C-suite executives see this happening way before it actually does.

Consider Coca-Cola. After the unsuccessful public reception of its "New Coke" in 1985—a move that risked alienating its core customer base—the company listened to its consumers, pivoted back to its original formula, rebranded it as "Coca-Cola Classic," and watched sales explode. The resurgence was so dramatic that Coca-Cola Classic sales doubled those of its biggest competitor, Pepsi, reestablishing the brand's dominance and proving the value of humility and adaptability.

Netflix, too, is a classic study in strategic pivoting. Originating as a DVD rental-by-mail company in the late 1990s, Netflix faced the looming obsolescence of physical media as streaming technology improved. Rather than clinging to its original, successful model, Netflix boldly transitioned to streaming, investing heavily in content-delivery networks and later, original content. This decision was not without risk—many doubted whether customers would be willing to change their viewing habits or trust in digital libraries. Yet, Netflix's willingness to pivot fundamentally altered how the world consumes entertainment and catapulted the company to global prominence.

Amazon's story is equally instructive. Starting as an online retailer that sold only books, the company's founder, Jeff Bezos, recognized the power of scale and the potential of e-commerce. Amazon expanded its offerings, launching the Amazon Marketplace, which allowed third-party vendors to sell on its platform. This not only diversified revenue streams but also turned Amazon into the "everything store." Today, Amazon is one of the largest companies in the world, with influence spanning retail, cloud computing, logistics, and more.

What unites these examples is not just a willingness to change, but an ability to recognize critical moments—inflection points—when a pivot is required. Successful businesses read the signals, let go of what no longer works, and pivot accordingly. Adaptability, far from being a buzzword, is a discipline and a mindset.

The Power Pivot for Business

"The Power Pivot for Business" isn't just a catchy phrase—it's a robust framework for strategic transformation, designed to empower organizations to adapt, innovate, and flourish amid relentless change. It enables companies to unlock new avenues for growth, build resilience in the face of adversity, and carve out lasting competitive advantages.

Transforming Challenges into Opportunities

In a world of constant disruption, economic shifts, technological advancements, and ever-evolving consumer behaviors continually reshape the business landscape. The ability to pivot strategically and with intention and clarity is no longer a luxury—it is an existential necessity, the key to survival and success. Society moves at the speed of light, and businesses that fail to keep up, risk being left behind, no matter how storied their past success.

The Power Pivot is about more than mere survival. It's about seizing new opportunities, even as you stay rooted in your organization's core values and vision. A true pivot is a deliberate, strategic shift—one that allows you to adapt, innovate, and thrive while staying authentic to your mission. It's not about abandoning your vision; it's about repositioning your business to capitalize on new possibilities while staying true to your purpose.

Case Study: X (formerly known as Twitter)

To illustrate the power of a pivot, look no further than the company now known as X. Twitter's origins trace back to Odeo, a podcasting platform founded in 2005. The model seemed promising—until Apple launched its own podcast platform via iTunes, effectively making Odeo irrelevant overnight. Rather than shutting down, Odeo's founders, Jack Dorsey and Biz Stone, assessed the landscape and recognized an emerging opportunity in microblogging. With remarkable agility, they pivoted to create Twitter in 2006.

From humble beginnings, Twitter rapidly gained traction, reaching 336 million users by 2018 and proving itself as a critical player in the global social media ecosystem.

Its valuation grew exponentially: at IPO, the company was valued at roughly $10 billion, and nine years later, when bought and rebranded as X by Elon Musk, it fetched a staggering $44 billion. This remarkable transformation took Odeo from a dying company to industry-defining innovation, all thanks to a timely and courageous pivot.

That pivot did more than save Odeo; it created a global tool for instantaneous communication, news dissemination, and social engagement, all born out of openness to change and a culture of employee-driven innovation.

So, whether it's X, Coca-Cola, Netflix, Amazon, or countless others, the willingness to read the market, understand changing realities, and flexibly course-correct—or *pivot*—enhances the odds of extraordinary success.

CHAPTER 8

THE THREE PILLARS OF EXECUTING

Just as with a Personal Power Pivot, there are three pillars to executing the Power Pivot for Business: Embracing Adaptive Leadership, Reimagining Your Value Proposition, and Building Agile Systems.

This next section is not just about you and your role in an organization, but how you can lead entire companies in their need to change and transition.

PILLAR 1: EMBRACE ADAPTIVE LEADERSHIP

I'll do a deeper dive on leadership in the third section of this book, but leadership and business go hand in hand. There's a reason embracing adaptive leadership is the first pillar of the Power Pivot for Business. Leadership is the cornerstone of any successful organizational transformation. In the fast-paced world of business, being a leader isn't about unyielding certainty or sticking rigidly to the plan—it's about adaptability, openness to change, and guiding your team with vision and courage through uncertainty.

Case Study: Netflix

Netflix's journey from DVD rentals to streaming giant is well-known, but its transformation was neither easy nor inevitable. In the early 2000s, Netflix was losing money, its model under threat from the omnipresent Blockbuster, which boasted over nine thousand retail locations worldwide. Netflix founders Reed Hastings and Marc Randolph saw where technology was headed—digital streaming. The two pitched Blockbuster on a partnership, which was resoundingly rejected. Hastings and Randolph had offered to sell their company to Blockbuster for $50 million, only to be dismissed. Blockbuster's CEO scoffed at the "dot-com hysteria," blind to the profound shift underway.[5] So, instead of clinging to their successful but fading model, Hastings and Randolph pivoted and doubled down on streaming technology, braving skepticism from investors and consumers. They invested heavily and transformed Netflix into a global entertainment powerhouse. Their adaptive leadership was crucial: it meant reading the signs, making tough calls, and charting a bold new path. Today, Netflix is worth over $540 billion, a testament to visionary leadership that isn't afraid to pivot.

---

5 Marc Randolph, *That Will Never Work: The Birth of Netflix and the Amazing Life of an Idea* (Little, Brown and Company, 2019), 251, Kindle.

Adaptive leadership hinges on three key principles:

1. **Anticipate Change.** Great leaders scan the horizon for trends—whether it's new technology, market shifts, or customer preferences. You must spend time and energy watching and studying what potentially may happen. Two examples of leaders who did this effectively are:

Satya Nadella

Satya Nadella of Microsoft, when he became CEO in 2014, foresaw the explosive growth of cloud computing and AI. He shifted Microsoft's focus from traditional software to cloud services (Azure) and AI, revitalizing the company and ensuring it led the next wave of tech innovation.

Elon Musk

Elon Musk anticipated and led the shift toward sustainable energy and electric vehicles, positioning Tesla to lead the EV market when others dismissed it and said it would never succeed. With SpaceX, Musk anticipated a new era of private-sector space exploration, pioneering reusable rockets and revolutionizing the market. He disrupted the aerospace industry by taking United States space exploration from the federal bureaucracy to the private sector.

Both Musk and Nadella combined vision, adaptability, and bold decision-making to stay ahead of industry trends, often reshaping their markets in the process. The lessons we take from them are to learn and know your market and industry so that you can predict future pivots, and in turn, you won't be left behind when trends start to change.

2. **Encourage your team to experiment, fail, and learn.** Adaptive leaders empower their teams to take risks, experiment, and learn from mistakes. Google's famous "20 percent time" policy allowed employees to work on passion projects for 20 percent of their on-the-clock time, giving birth to groundbreaking products like Gmail and Google Maps. Shopify, the e-commerce platform, embodies this philosophy by encouraging developers to experiment—even with so-called "throwaway" work—fostering a culture of constant learning.

Case Study: Shopify

Encouraging empowerment highlights Shopify's culture of experimentation and learning from failure—a cornerstone of its ability to innovate and scale rapidly. The company grew from Gross Merchandise Volume (GMV) of $26 billion in 2017 to a cumulative Gross Merchandise Volume of almost $200 billion by 2021. I found Shopify's story so compelling that I went a little deeper on how they encourage this way of working. You can find an even deeper dive of this story in several books: *The Shopify Story: How a Startup Rocketed to E-commerce Giant by Empowering Millions of Entrepreneurs* by Larry MacDonald, and *Shopify: The Book I Wish I Had Read Before Launching my Store* by Patrice Audet.

Shopify's Framework for Structured Experimentation:

- **Host a Growth Workshop for Cross-Functional Innovation.** Create a growth workshop, including a multidisciplinary team across departments, to coordinate new ideas and experimentation.

- **Hack Days for Bottom-Up Innovation.** All employees can work on any project they choose.
- **Encourage Data-Driven Learning and Utilize Analytics.** Using data as a tool for learning—both from successes and failures.
- **Foster Psychological Safety and a Culture of Learning.** Leadership destigmatizes failure, encourages employees to take risks, and agrees not to punish them for mistakes.
- **Choose Long-Term Vision Over Short-Term Metrics.** The culture is driven by a long-term vision rather than short-term success.
- **Employ External Partnerships to Scale Experimentation.** Using outside resources helps with cost and lowers the chance of failure.
- **Learn from the Shopify Academy for Continuous Learning**. Leadership trains employees and uses outside resources to help with consistent and regular team education.

Experimentation isn't always, "Let's throw something on the wall and see what sticks." It also isn't lacking structure or organization. In fact, being experimental and achieving successful results is defined and easily embedded into your core operations.

3. **Make Big, Bold Decisions.**

Adaptive leaders don't shy away from tough calls. An example of this is when Starbucks faced declining sales in 2008, CEO Howard Schultz pivoted by closing underperforming stores, retraining staff, and refocusing on customer experience.

Within a year, Starbucks' stock recovered, gaining 143 percent from its lows.

Similarly, when Alan Mulally took the helm at Ford in 2006, he bet big on a turnaround. By 2008, Ford was facing bankruptcy during the financial crisis. Mulally implemented some bold policies. The One Ford Strategy streamlined operations, mortgaged almost all of Ford's assets by borrowing $23.6 billion, and redid its culture to help encourage transparency. The result was a revitalized company that survived the financial crisis and saw its stock price nearly double from less than eight dollars a share to fifteen dollars a share between 2006 and 2014.

Adaptive leadership is the bedrock of the Power Pivot for Business. It's about staying anchored in your vision while being flexible enough to navigate—and even shape—future change.

PILLAR 2: REIMAGINE YOUR VALUE

The second pillar of the Power Pivot for Business is Reimagining Your Value. In a dynamic market, what worked yesterday may not work tomorrow, and definitely not in five to ten years. A Power Pivot requires rethinking how you deliver value to meet the changing world. How do you continue to run your company every day but also anticipate what is coming down the pike?

When pivoting, a business must reimagine its value. It's not always easy, but it's always necessary. I have outlined tools to systematically explore new opportunities, test changes, and ensure alignment with both company goals and evolving customer needs.

A Toolbox for Reimagining Your Value:

- **Test Small, Learn Fast.** Experiment to learn from failures without excessive costs. Make minor changes that don't risk your bottom line before going "all in."
- **Stay Customer-Focused.** Validate pivots with real customer feedback to ensure you're solving actual needs.
- **Balance Risk.** Avoid over-pivoting by testing long-term impacts.
- **Align with Vision.** Make sure changes are consistent with your long-term purpose and goals.

These tools will help you rethink value while minimizing risks through experimentation.

Case Study: Airbnb

In 2007, Airbnb's founders Brian Chesky and Joe Gebbia rented out an air mattress in their small apartment to help pay rent, launching what would become Air Bed and Breakfast, which of course, later became Airbnb. They soon partnered with Nathan Blecharczyk, and the three pivoted their platform from "cheap lodging" to "unique, local experiences," expecting the rise of the sharing economy. Their vision allowed Airbnb to grow into a global hospitality powerhouse worth approximately $81 billion, transforming travel and accommodation.

Case Study: Instagram

Instagram began as Burbn, an app overloaded with features—location check-ins, gaming, and photo sharing. Early on, founders Kevin Systrom and Mike Krieger realized they were offering too many different things and people weren't using Burbn. They noticed users were primarily engaging with the photo-sharing feature, so Systrom and Krieger stripped Burbn to focus solely on that. They rebranded as Instagram in 2010. Once they pivoted, Instagram exploded in popularity, amassing more users in a day than Burbn had in a year. Within two years, Facebook bought Instagram for $300 million and 23 million shares of stock.[6] Today, Instagram boasts over two billion active monthly users, showing how reimagining value can unlock massive growth.

PILLAR 3: BUILD THINGS YOU CAN CHANGE

The third pillar of the Power Pivot is building things you can change.

A true pivot isn't just a one-time decision; it's a skill you can use repeatedly that enables flexibility, efficiency, and innovation. This means creating business models, systems, and workflows that allow for rapid experimentation and scaling. Additionally, emotional attachment can't complicate the business need.

How to Build Things You Can Change:

- **Leverage Technology.** Continuing our Airbnb example, the company built a modular platform with APIs (Application Programming Interface) to integrate new features and adapt to changing demands. They used data analytics to track user behavior, identifying demand for remote work accommodations. The company's tech

6 Emil Protalinski, "Facebook buying Instagram for $300 million, 23 million shares," *ZD Net*, April 23, 2012, https://www.zdnet.com/article/facebook-buying-instagram-for-300-million-23-million-shares/.

infrastructure enabled quick pivots, like shifting to long-term stays in 2020 during the COVID-19 pandemic when travel plummeted. Data and AI ensured offerings matched user needs, while experiments validated new markets. Using a flexible platform enabled Airbnb to quickly make changes as data was driving real world results.

- **Create flexible processes.** Build a business that can adapt to change, create flexible processes using these simple strategies:
    - **Make Processes Modular.** Break workflows into independent parts so you can adjust one without disrupting others.
    - **Test and Learn.** Try new workflows on a small scale, set clear success metrics, and refine based on results.
    - **Use Tech to Automate.** Automate repetitive tasks. Use automation to free up human resources for innovation.
    - **Encourage Feedback**. Create regular feedback loops with employees.

One example of this is how Toast CEO Aman Narang designed his business with the ability to make quick changes. If you aren't familiar with Toast, it's a restaurant technology platform that was working with restaurants on, among other things, contactless payments and reservations prior to the pandemic. Toast's modular APIs and propensity for rapid experimentation allowed it to pivot quickly from reservations to delivery and takeout when the pandemic shut down dining rooms. By 2022, Toast reached a $30 billion valuation, supporting thousands of independent restaurants through turbulent times. It was a substantial change from their original, pre-2019 business model.

Toast was able to use data and industry information to make change.

Below are ways for you to build a business that can adapt by using data and industry information:

1. Track Customer Data
2. Stay Informed on Trends.
3. Predict Future Needs.
4. Use Constructive Feedback from peers or competitors.

Now that you know the three pillars for business, use them to help execute your Power Pivot. Together, they provide a blueprint for businesses to navigate uncertainty, capitalize on new opportunities, and thrive in ever-evolving markets.

Let's dig into the blueprint.

CHAPTER 9

INTRODUCTION TO THE POWER PIVOT BLUEPRINT

As the business landscape shifts at unprecedented speed, the ability to pivot—swiftly and strategically—has become essential for any organization looking not just to survive, but to thrive. Whether confronted by disruptive technology, evolving customer needs, or emerging competitors, today's leaders must be ready to steer their companies through uncertainty with agility, vision, and confidence. This chapter introduces the Power Pivot for Business framework: a practical, four-step blueprint designed to help you transform challenges into opportunities, drive sustainable growth, and secure a lasting competitive edge. By integrating adaptive leadership, a reimagined value proposition, and agile systems, you'll discover how to systematically assess your business, define and launch focused pivots, and build a culture of accountability and learning that empowers your team to boldly shape the future.

Bringing It All Together: Your Power Pivot Plan

As mentioned above and throughout the past two chapters, this framework integrates the three pillars—Embracing Adaptive Leadership, Reimagining Your Value Proposition, and Building Agile Systems—into a four-step process.

Step 1: Assess Your Current State

We can never move forward if we don't take a good hard look at where we are. With that in mind, conduct what I call a "pivot audit"—an overall audit to show where your business is stuck. Here's how:

- **Analyze market trends.** Look at all customer feedback and your financial performance.
- **Identify threats.** Who are your new competitors? What technological shifts and opportunities are developing?
- **Use data to pinpoint inefficiencies or outdated processes.** Use SWOT analysis (Strengths, Weaknesses, Opportunities, Threats) to map your landscape and chart a path forward. Its purpose is to put in writing your overall goals in addition to an outline of your current situation. Spend time and effort on the process; it will give you the clearest picture of where your business stands and what needs to change.

Step 2: Define Your Pivot

Choose one specific, strategic shift that aligns with your core values and long-term vision. The change can be minor, or it can be major, but finding out what you need to do is half the battle. The key here is defining your pivot and focusing on just that one, whether it be a new product, market, or business model. Then break out the "Reimagine Your Value" tools:

- **Test Small, Learn Fast.** Run low-cost experiments to validate ideas.
- **Stay Customer-Focused.** They're the lifeblood of any business. Never lose sight of that.
- **Balance Risk.** Assess long-term impacts to avoid over-pivoting.
- **Align with Vision.** Ensure the pivot supports your mission.

Suggested Tools:

Create a one-page pivot proposal outlining the shift, goals, and metrics for success—a focused pivot that leverages opportunities while staying true to your purpose and core values.

Step 3: Launch a Ninety-Day Sprint

Execute your pivot with a structured, time-bound plan to test and refine it. Here's what you do:

- **Set clear, measurable goals**. Something like, "increase revenue by 10 percent" or "acquire one thousand new users."

- **Assign responsibilities to team members and align resources.** Delegate and assign. Create a shared vision.
- **Implement Adaptive Leadership Principles.** Be willing to change directions when something isn't working.
- **Anticipate Change.** Monitor trends to stay ahead.
- **Encourage Experimentation.** Allow teams to test and learn from failures.
- **Make Bold Decisions.** Act decisively to drive the pivot.
- **Track progress weekly with data-driven metrics.** Remember Airbnb's pivot to long-term stays during the pandemic and how they were able to rapidly test using their modular platform and data analytics.

Suggested Tools:

Use a project management tool like Trello or Asana to track tasks, deadlines, and key metrics.

Step 4: Build Accountability and Learning

Create systems to sustain the changes and foster continuous improvement. How to do this:

- **Leverage Agile Systems.** Make change easy but not getting stuck in immoveable structure.
- **Build Modular Processes.** This makes it easy to make changes with recreating everything from the beginning.
- **Design workflows that can be adjusted independently.** Don't be bogged down in bureaucratic approvals.
- **Test and Learn.** Run small-scale experiments with clear success metrics.

- **Automate with Tech.** Use tools like APIs or AI to streamline operations.
- **Encourage Feedback.** Set up regular feedback loops with employees and customers.
- **Use data.** Track behavior, industry trends, and pivot outcomes.
- **Foster a culture of psychological safety.** Encourage risk-taking and learning from failures.

Let's use the example of Shopify's experimentation culture and how it enabled rapid scaling and innovation. Remember how culture grew the company at a record speed over four to five years. The key is designing ways to implement a feedback dashboard to collect and analyze employee and customer input based on the "experiments" you're conducting. This requires a flexible, data-driven business capable of repeated pivots.

I would like to end this chapter with a few of the methods I've used in helping companies and CEOs reach success. It's a summary of what's outlined above in five key areas:

1. **Stay Proactive.** Anticipate market shifts before they force change (example: Satya Nadella's early bet on cloud and AI at Microsoft).
2. **Keep It Simple.** Focus on one pivot at a time to avoid overwhelming you or your team and drive clarity.
3. **Use Data.** Leverage analytics to validate decisions and forecast future needs.
4. **Lead with Courage.** Embrace big, bold moves, as seen with Starbucks' store closures or Ford's $23.6 billion loan.

5. **Iterate Continuously.** Treat pivots as an ongoing discipline, not just a crisis response or one-time fix.

The Power Is in Your Pivot

I want to remind you that the Power Pivot is not about reacting to change—it's about proactively shaping the future. Netflix didn't just survive the shift from DVDs to streaming; it redefined entertainment. Airbnb didn't just adapt to the sharing economy; it created an entirely new way to experience travel. Instagram wasn't just another failed app; it became a centerpiece of digital culture.

These companies thrived because they embraced their Power Pivot. They seized the moment, reimagined their value, and built systems that could support ongoing evolution. Your business, regardless of its size or stage, has the same potential. You don't need a radical overhaul overnight. Sometimes, a single, strategic pivot—rooted in adaptive leadership, a reimagined value proposition, or agile systems—can set you on a path to extraordinary growth and resilience.

THE POWER PIVOT

LEADERSHIP

asset were valued. I had several conversations with other firms of similar size that experienced a comparable situation. In these conversations, I learned the potential pitfalls and benefits that could come from selling the firm.

These meetings were a masterclass in valuation, the mechanics of deal structure, the emotional calculus of letting go, and, most importantly, the challenge of integrating teams and cultures. Some stories were cautionary—founders who regretted losing their autonomy, teams that fractured under new management—but others shared tales of renewal and growth where joining with another firm brought new opportunities and energy. I listened, asked questions, and took careful notes, all while quietly assessing what would work for us.

One night I ran into one of my now-partners at a Washington restaurant beside the Capitol. Matt Bravo was at S.E. Group, a firm we'd been collaborating with for years. We shared clients and intelligence, and their leadership, John Scofield and Mike Fuentes, were trusted friends. Others at West Front Strategies were also friends and business associates with various members of the S.E. team. From that brief encounter with Bravo, a seed was planted.

It was a serendipitous meeting that felt almost fated—two teams with overlapping networks, shared values, and a shared vision for the future of government affairs. During the next several months, our conversations deepened, moving from polite [illegible] talk about [illegible] that the [illegible] [illegible] I realized that our [illegible] [illegible]

CHAPTER 10

GOOD LEADERS PIVOT

We live in a quick-paced world of perpetual change. We see it in daily economic shifts, political change, and technological advancements—artificial intelligence is changing the world as we know it every minute of every hour of every day. We're constantly awakening to something new—the speed of information and the ability to adapt to change is a constant challenge. For anyone in leadership, the curveballs don't just test your skills; they test your soul. They trigger existential questions whose answers hold the keys to transformative change and the willingness to drive change as you lead others.

Ask yourself: How do you stay steady when the ground shifts? How do you inspire others when you're not sure what's around the corner? Tough questions to be sure, but necessary. I've sat in boardrooms with "Fortune 500" executives as the markets crashed and worked with government leaders during national crises, and what I've learned is this: The difference between those who crumble and those who thrive isn't luck or talent; it's the ability to see when you need to change—not just react, but strategically shift your mindset, your actions, and your vision to seize the moment before it is defined for you.

As I have said throughout this book, intentional planning leads to intentional change. Whether it is for yourself, your business, or leading others, anticipation and direction is what leads to the success. The framework to succeed isn't a concept, it's a practical roadmap to unlock your potential, turn adversity into opportunity, and to lead with purpose. Whether you're leading a team, building a career, or simply trying to figure out what's next, this is about empowering you to take control of the story.

In the Power Pivot for Leadership, recognizing, reframing, and redirecting are key steps for navigating challenges, making decisions, and leading effectively. They empower you to strategically shift perspectives and actions. Let's break down each area with a few live examples along the way.

- **Recognize.** You must acknowledge the current situation, emotions, or challenges objectively. How and why do you want to lead your team or organization to make a change? This involves recognizing what's happening, understanding the context, and being aware of your own biases or emotional reactions. It's about clearly seeing reality without denial or distortion of what you want it to look like.
- **Reframe.** You must shift your perspective by reinterpreting the situation to find new meaning and opportunities. This step involves challenging your assumption of what you *think* you know by looking at the problem

from different angles and finding a constructive way to view it.

Example: Instead of seeing disengagement as a lack of effort, a leader reframes it as a sign the team needs clearer goals or more meaningful tasks.

- **Redirect.** To move forward effectively, you must act based on your newfound perspective. This involves adjusting strategies, behaviors, or communication to align with the reframed understanding to achieve better outcomes.

Together, these steps help you as a leader pause, reassess, and act thoughtfully to turn challenges into opportunities for growth and progress. My belief that these steps can lead us where we want to go was confirmed after I read *My Life in Full: Work, Family, and Our Future*, the memoir of the former CEO of PepsiCo, Indra Nooyi. I realized she used these steps during her tenure as CEO, and more than likely before that in other leadership positions at the company.

Case Study: PepsiCo.

Nooyi *recognized, reframed,* and *redirected* during a crucial time for her industry and PepsiCo. In the early 2000s, it became clear that consumer preferences were changing toward healthier products. Nooyi recognized the risk of relying heavily on sugary drinks and snacks. She realized she needed to lead a strategic pivot in and with her company or risk losing significant market share. Nooyi saw the shifting consumer landscape by seeing several critical indicators:

- **Market Trends.** Nooyi noted growing consumer awareness of health and wellness, with increasing demand for low-sugar, low-fat, and natural products, driven by rising obesity concerns and health campaigns.
- **Data Analysis.** As a strategic leader, Nooyi leveraged market research and sales data showing declining soda consumption and a rise in healthier beverage and snack categories, such as bottled water and whole-grain products.
- **Stakeholder Feedback.** Nooyi listened to customer feedback, retailer insights, and societal pressures highlighting the negative health impacts of sugary drinks and processed snacks.
- **Competitive Landscape.** Nooyi observed competitors like Coca-Cola and smaller health-focused brands gaining traction with healthier offerings, which signaled a market shift.

By synthesizing these signals, Nooyi recognized PepsiCo's heavy reliance on traditional, less-healthy products as a potential long-term risk, prompting her to start the "Performance with Purpose" strategy to diversify into healthier options like Quaker Oats and Tropicana.

After Nooyi *recognized* the shift toward healthier consumer preferences, she had to *reframe* PepsiCo's role from solely a snack and soda company to a diversified company selling "better-for-you" products, aligning with health trends to drive growth for the bottom line of the company.

Below is an example of how Nooyi reframed PepsiCo through the four-point strategy *I* use when I want to reframe a situation or position.

1. **Challenge Existing Assumptions.** Nooyi had to question PepsiCo's traditional identity as a leader in sugary drinks and snacks. She saw that clinging to this model could limit future growth as consumer preferences shifted toward health-conscious choices.
2. **Adopt a Broader Perspective.** Nooyi reframed PepsiCo's mission from solely delivering indulgent products to providing a balanced portfolio that included healthier options.
3. **Engage Stakeholders.** Nooyi consulted with internal teams, nutrition experts, and market analysts to understand how PepsiCo could innovate while maintaining profitability. This helped her view health trends as an opportunity to lead rather than a threat. This is crucial in leadership—learning how to change a challenge into something that can make you a better leader.
4. **Identify Opportunities.** Nooyi saw the growing health and wellness market as a chance to expand PepsiCo's portfolio, buy health-focused brands, and innovate new products, rather than being constrained by declining sales in unhealthy food.

Through this guide I use for leadership, I showed you how Nooyi transformed the challenge of changing consumer preferences into an opportunity to reposition PepsiCo as a forward-thinking, diversified food and beverage company. It's a great exercise for you to do as well if you're looking to lead through a challenge or a change.

The last step in the Power Pivot for Leadership is to *redirect.* I consider this the most important step in the exercise because it means taking action—putting a plan in place after you've done all the hard work in seeing what needs to happen to be successful. *Recognize* and *reframe* are the organization, and *redirect* is the action.

If we stay with Nooyi and PepsiCo as the example, her process of reframing and recognizing the need to turn the company into a health-conscious brand, she redirected PepsiCo by investing in healthier product lines, restructuring marketing, and launching sustainability initiatives under "Performance with Purpose." This is a breakdown of how Nooyi used this blueprint for redirection. Her model doesn't fit every challenge, but the overall thought process is something worth noting.

- **Portfolio Diversification.** Shifted resources to expand PepsiCo's healthy product lines by buying brands that fit that goal.
- **Research and Development Investment.** Redirected research and development efforts to focus on reformulating products to reduce health risks.
- **Marketing Realignment.** Changed marketing strategies to emphasize PepsiCo's healthier offerings and sustainability efforts.
- **Cultural and Organizational Shifts.** Encouraged a company-wide mindset shift by aligning leadership and employees with the new vision.
- **Stakeholder Engagement.** Engaged investors, customers, and partners to build support for the strategic pivot.

The entire blueprint underscores the critical importance of adaptability for effective leadership in a rapidly changing world. Using the example of Indra Nooyi's transformation of PepsiCo in response to shifting consumer preferences, I illustrate how leaders must objectively assess their environment, challenge assumptions, and take decisive action aligned with a new vision. Nooyi's approach, which included diversifying PepsiCo's portfolio, investing in healthier products, and realigning company culture, exemplifies how intentional planning and strategic pivots can empower leaders to guide their organizations through uncertainty and drive purposeful growth.

In the months following the merger, we found that these small, deliberate adjustments in how we conducted team meetings, onboarded clients, and checked in with one another had outsized impact. They paved the way for [illegible] and forged a new collective identity that was stronger than the sum of its parts.

Now the question is: how do you incorporate the changes you're making into your broader Power Pivot?

These are examples of what I've used to make my Tiny Pivots effective:

- *Align with Your Why.* Ensure each Tiny Pivot ties directly to your overarching Power Pivot goal to keep focused.
- *Start Small.* Choose actions so easy you can't fail (for example, "read one page" instead of "read a book").
- *Use Triggers.* Tie Tiny Pivots with existing habits (for example, meditating for two minutes after brushing your teeth).
- *Stay Flexible.* If a Tiny Pivot isn't working, tweak it rather than abandoning the entire goal.
- *Leverage Community.* Share your Tiny Pivots with a friend or group for accountability. (For example, you could post your progress on social media or tell friends your goal and how you are doing.)

It's important to remember that Tiny Pivots are not about settling for less—they're about making progress visible and sustainable. The satisfaction of progress, no matter how incremental, generates more momentum for the next step.

CHAPTER 11

DEEPENING THE FRAMEWORK: WHY GOOD LEADERS MUST PIVOT

Before we do a deep dive into the "whys" of leadership pivots, I want to walk through how I used the model in the last chapter to make recent changes in my life. It's something that was extremely helpful in developing clarity while making change. First, I want to give you two more fun examples of companies with forward thinking leadership who pivoted their companies through situations to survive.

Why Pivoting Makes a Good Leader

The ability to pivot is more than a skill—it's a mindset cultivated through practice, humility, and a willingness to let go of what no longer serves you or your organization. Good leaders know that resistance to change often comes from fear: fear of losing control, fear of the unknown, or fear of failure. The art of the pivot is in recognizing these fears but not allowing them to rule you. Instead, great leaders use them as signals, guiding where attention and energy must flow to create new value.

A good pivot is not a reckless leap, but a calculated step. It requires the courage to pause, the wisdom to assess, and the discipline to act with conviction even when certainty is elusive.

When leaders embrace the pivot, they model adaptability and resilience for their teams. They communicate openly about why change is necessary, listen actively to concerns, and invite collaboration in shaping the path forward. They acknowledge uncertainty but keep a precise vision, helping others to see not only the risk of change, but also its promise.

The best pivots are not *re*active; they are *pro*active. Leaders who are always scanning the horizon, learning, and iterating position themselves and their organizations to seize opportunities early, often before competitors even realize a shift is underway.

The Emotional Intelligence of the Pivot

Change is not just strategic—it's profoundly emotional. For many, the prospect of pivoting can bring anxiety, confusion, or even grief for what is being left behind. Good leaders are attuned to these undercurrents. They foster psychological safety, encouraging open dialogue and supporting their teams through the discomfort that comes with transformation. This human-centered approach enables deeper commitment and creativity as a leader forges new direction.

In my own experience, the leaders who navigated pivots most effectively were those who could connect the "why" of change to a shared sense of purpose, making the transition feel meaningful rather than arbitrary. They celebrated small wins, acknowledged setbacks honestly, and kept momentum alive by reinforcing a sense of possibility.

Case Studies: Pivoting in Action

Case Study: Sweetgreen

Jonathan Neman, CEO of the fast-casual salad restaurant Sweetgreen, applied the Power Pivot Framework for Leaders (recognize, reframe, redirect) to navigate challenges and drive the company's growth. The pandemic was a tough time for the chain, and change needed to happen.

- **Recognize.** Neman identified key challenges affecting Sweetgreen's business model. Post-pandemic, he acknowledged publicly that urban store locations, heavily reliant on office traffic, were underperforming, with only 50 percent of pre-pandemic traffic returning. There was also a rise in labor costs, a change in consumer preferences, and a need for scalability as Sweetgreen prepared for an IPO and expansion.
- **Reframe.** Neman knew he needed to shift his perspective, viewing these challenges as opportunities. Instead of focusing solely on urban markets, he saw potential in

suburban expansion where population growth was surging. And my favorite example: Neman decided to use more automation—not just as a cost-cutting gimmick, but to enhance efficiency and employee experience.

- **Redirect**. As the CEO, Neman took decisive and quick action to align Sweetgreen with this reframed vision. This is what he did:
  - **Suburban Expansion.** Expanded most of his new store investments outside of cities and into growing suburban areas.
  - **Automation (Infinite Kitchen).** Implemented robotic assembly systems in select locations, increasing output to 500 meals per hour, improving profit margins (28 percent versus 18 percent in traditional stores), and reducing employee turnover by enhancing work conditions.
  - **Menu Diversification.** Introduced protein options like steak and salmon to attract more male customers and boost dinnertime sales.
  - **Operational Streamlining.** Professionalized his back-office management and technology making sure he was in line with what it takes for a company to go public.

Case Study: YouTube

This truly is my favorite example of any company I've ever studied. The original concept for YouTube, created by founders Steve Chen, Chad Hurley, and Jawed Karim in February 2005, was not solely as a general video-sharing platform. It was originally meant to be a dating site, complete with the slogan, "Tune In,

Hook Up," where users could upload a video to connect romantically. Chen, Hurley, and Karim quickly realized that people weren't really using their platform for dating but to share videos. Applying the Power Pivot Framework (recognize, reframe, redirect) is how the founders, particularly Hurley, as the first CEO, made YouTube what it is today.

- **Recognize.** Hurley and the founders quickly identified that the dating-focused video platform idea wasn't gaining traction. User engagement was low, and feedback showed people were uploading a variety of videos beyond dating, such as personal vlogs and entertainment clips. They recognized the limitations of the niche dating concept and the broader potential for video-sharing in a rapidly growing internet landscape.
- **Reframe.** The founders shifted their perspective, reframing YouTube's purpose from a dating-specific platform to a universal video-sharing hub. They saw the lack of dating video uploads not as a failure but as an opportunity to create a platform where anyone could share any type of video, tapping into the internet's demand for user-generated content and self-expression.
- **Redirect.** Hurley and the team took quick divisive actions to pivot YouTube's strategy, which was:
    - **Platform Redesign.** They scrapped the dating focus and relaunched YouTube in 2005 as an open platform for all types of video content.
    - **User Engagement.** They simplified the interface and added features like comments and playlists to encourage broader user participation.

- **Infrastructure Scaling.** They invested in server capacity to handle diverse video uploads.
- **Profit Opportunity.** They began exploring ad-based revenue models to sustain the platform.

Through this process, the founders pivoted YouTube from a struggling dating app concept to a revolutionary video-sharing platform.

I wonder how many of you remember when it was a dating app????

Personal Tools for Effective Pivoting

As I close this chapter, I want to leave you with four personal tools that I use when I am thinking about a change and need to lead others in doing so.

1. **Remove yourself from your comfort zone by taking risks.** There is absolutely no way you will get to where you want to be or to the next level if you are not willing to take a risk. Good leaders understand that calculated risks are essential to unlocking new growth and discovery. Each new challenge brings fresh perspectives—and often, unexpected solutions.
2. **Be comfortable with being uncomfortable.** Every seven days, push yourself into doing something uncomfortable. The concept of doing something uncomfortable every seven days doesn't appear to have a single, definitive originator, but the idea aligns with contemporary trends in psychology and personal growth that show stepping out of one's comfort zone fosters resilience, growth, or

habit change. Over time, this practice expands your comfort zone and enhances your leadership agility.

3. **Turn confidence into courage.** Just because you have confidence in what you do doesn't necessarily mean you have the courage to make a change. Courage is the willingness to act in the face of uncertainty, to challenge the status quo, and to inspire others to do the same. Leadership demands not only belief in oneself, but the tenacity to step forward when the outcome is unknown.
4. **Do the hard work.** No explanation needed. Consistent, persistent effort is the foundation of every successful pivot. The most effective leaders roll up their sleeves and do what needs to be done, setting a powerful example for those around them.

Here's the secret sauce of the Power Pivot: when you pivot, you give others permission to do the same. I've seen it in teams I've led and in audiences to whom I've spoken. When you model resilience, adaptability, and purpose, it spreads.

The biggest thing I've learned about leadership is that people are watching. They watch how you act, how you treat people, how you treat yourself, and how you handle a crisis. At fifty, I do these things much differently than I did at twenty-five, thirty-five, or even forty-five. I continue to learn and grow and watch people I admire make difficult changes.

Think about the people you lead—your employees, your family, and your community. What would happen if they saw you turn a setback into a steppingstone? That's leadership at its best—not just solving problems, but inspiring others to rise. Leadership is about encouraging them to make changes and giving them the space to make mistakes and eventually create something bigger and better.

Reflection Questions

- When was the last time you recognized a need to pivot in your leadership or life? What signals did you notice?
- How did you reframe the challenge to see new possibilities? Who did you engage for perspective?
- What actions did you take to redirect your efforts? What was the outcome?
- How did your pivot inspire or influence others around you?

Change is inevitable. Growth is not. It's your pivots—the ones you make intentionally and with courage—that shape your legacy as a leader. Let the stories and strategies from this chapter serve as both compass and encouragement as you chart your own course through change.

THE POWER PIVOT

THE TIME IS NOW

CHAPTER 12

TINY PIVOTS

In the context of the Power Pivot, I've shared significant, intentional shifts in one's life direction, mindset, and behavior to achieve a transformative goal. I've offered up ways in which to lead a significant Power Pivot for your team, family, or company. The Power Pivot is a bold, strategic move that requires commitment and often involves multiple steps to reach your final goal.

As I was writing this book, I realized that I'm in the middle of another major pivot in my life, although I'm not sure what it is or what the outcome will be. Nevertheless, I've recognized that I have been making little (and some big) changes over the past two years to set me on a path to where I want to go next. When I started writing, I began calling what I've been doing the past few years "Tiny Pivots." At first, I was sort of joking by calling them that, but then I decided to research what Tiny Pivots mean in the context a serious life change.

The Nature and Power of Tiny Pivots

Here's what I found:

Tiny Pivots are small, incremental adjustments or actions that contribute to the larger Power Pivot. They are deliberate, manageable changes that build momentum, create habits, and gradually align you with your goal.

Tiny Pivots are micro-changes that support the overarching goal of your Power Pivot.

What I love about them is that they are:

- **Low-risk and achievable.** Small enough to feel doable.
- **Consistent and compounding.** Repeated over time, they build progress toward the larger shift.
- **Aligned with the goal.** Each Tiny Pivot moves you closer to the desired outcome of the Power Pivot.
- **Adaptable.** They allow for course correction based on feedback or changing circumstances. If something isn't working, then change it and try something new.

It's the compounding effect of these micro-shifts that make Tiny Pivots so powerful. Each one, almost invisible on its own, becomes a building block in constructing a new reality. Over weeks and months, what seem like small, inconsequential changes—opting for a ten-minute walk after lunch, exchanging a nightly scroll through social media for a chapter of a book, or spending Sundays mapping out the week—grow into powerful habits that reshape the ordinary course of your life.

Often, we become fixated on the idea that only dramatic, sweeping action will move the needle. But in truth, few people can overhaul their lives overnight, and those who do often struggle with the sustainability of such abrupt change. Tiny Pivots, by contrast, are sustainable. They accumulate, layer by layer, until you look up and realize that you are, in fact, living a different life than you were just a year prior.

Practical Examples of Tiny Pivots

To bring this to life, consider the example of someone looking to transition from a corporate job to starting their own business. Tiny Pivots in this scenario might include:

- Spending ten minutes each evening researching business ideas, gradually building a list of what excites them
- Reaching out to one new person each week who has experience as an entrepreneur, forging connections and gaining insights
- Setting aside one lunch hour a week to read books or articles about successful business launches, keeping inspiration and learning fresh
- Testing a small side project on weekends to experiment with business concepts in a low-pressure environment
- Developing a habit of jotting down observations about their strengths, interests, and values every morning

These actions, while individually modest, create a rhythm of progress. More importantly, they make the Power Pivot feel less overwhelming and more attainable. By dividing the journey into digestible steps, the individual keeps momentum even on days when motivation wanes or uncertainty looms large.

The Subtle Art of Self-Discovery

Tiny Pivots also invite self-discovery. Because they are small and adaptable, you can safely experiment, learn, and adjust course. If the pivot you tried doesn't feel right, it's easy to recalibrate without the weight of "failure." This adaptability is what makes Tiny Pivots so effective over the long run; they create a culture of curiosity and resilience.

Turning Fifty: My Personal Tiny Pivots

I would like to share with you Tiny Pivots that I have been working through and spending lots of time perfecting over the past twenty-four months, which are in the context of turning fifty this past January. I knew it was a big milestone in not only age, but also my career and where my family was in our journey. Ideas and thoughts started creeping into my head of what that means, like, "How do I start thinking about what fifty, fifty-three, and fifty-five look like in where I want to be professionally and personally?" I started strategizing during my "5AM Club" mornings the entire year leading up to turning fifty as well as the whole year of being fifty. I decided there were a few major overall goals I wanted to achieve.

Individual Goals

- Do more paid public speaking.
- Do something that will help me grow personally and professionally and that makes me a little bit nervous.

- Spend as much time with my family as possible. (Oliver was turning sixteen, and I just began to realize that there were only two years left before he went to college.)

Business Goals

- Figure out where I think the firm my partners and I started almost ten years ago is going next. Do we need to add more people, sell, or merge?

Leadership Needs and Goals

- Look for opportunities to grow the firm to the next level and grow me as well.

As I reflect on the past two years and look ahead to the next chapter, I'm reminded that the journey of change is just as important as the destination. By honoring and intentionally crafting each Tiny Pivot, you give yourself permission to evolve—one small, meaningful move at a time.

Let's look at what I have been up to and how I have used the Power Pivot model for my little pivots as well.

Personal Tiny Pivot

The Tiny Pivots I've been making over the past two years began as ideas which percolated—sometimes quietly, sometimes insistently—until they demanded attention and action. At first, these were just fleeting thoughts, nudges in the back of my mind that, just maybe, I was ready for a new direction. They led me to put together a plan and, more importantly, to implement it. It's been said that a dream without a plan is just a wish, and I've found truth in that statement. There is something quietly powerful about moving from daydreaming to intentional goal setting. So instead of simply wishing for change, I made the decision to set a tangible goal and map out the steps to achieve it.

In this case, it was the realization that I wanted to expand my professional life into the realm of paid public speaking. While I had ample experience and comfort with topics like politics, policy, and elections—subjects I have lived, breathed, and debated for years—I found myself yearning for something different. I wanted to develop a speech that moved beyond the news cycle, something resonant and enduring, something that could outlast any single election or political moment.

Of course, this was not a simple pivot. I needed to build a speech that could hold an audience for forty-five to sixty minutes, keeping them engaged, provoked, and inspired. There is a delicate art to this—crafting a narrative arc, threading together anecdotes, insights, and lessons that draw people in and leave them with something to take home. I wanted to offer ideas and stories that were both deeply personal and widely relevant.

BigSpeak Speakers Bureau, where I am fortunate enough to be a paid speaker, pointed me toward ImpactEleven, a firm known for helping speakers refine and reinvent their messages. Their encouragement planted a seed that grew into something new—something I felt uniquely equipped to share. This is how the concept of the Power Pivot was born: not as a dramatic overhaul of my life or profession, but as a series of small, deliberate shifts, each one pushing me a little further out of my comfort zone and a little closer to the kind of impact I wanted to make.

I spent more than six months in deep reflection, asking myself what I truly had to offer. What could I share with authority and authenticity? What stories from my own journey—mistakes, successes, and unexpected turns—could illuminate the path for others? There were plenty of false starts and moments of self-doubt. It's easy to be the expert in what you know; it's much harder to be vulnerable, to chart a new course, and to do it publicly. I describe this as a "Tiny Pivot" because, in the grand scheme, it may seem a modest change, but for me, it was a monumental act of self-direction. It was a conscious decision to grow, to stretch, and to try something I had never done before.

When I look back now, I realize that this Tiny Pivot is the reason I'm writing this book at all. The process of developing a new speech, of sharing my personal stories and perspectives in a public forum, opened something in me. It has reminded me that growth often comes not from seismic shifts, but from a series of small, intentional steps. I am genuinely pleased with the opportunities that have come my way so far, but I am also aware that I am still learning, still evolving, and that the journey is far from over. There is more growing to do, more pivots to make.

CHAPTER 13

HOW TINY PIVOTS LEAD TO BIG TRANSFORMATION

The first step in making my Tiny Pivot—recognizing what needed to change—took longer than I'd care to admit. The public speaking industry itself is vast, valued at over $6 billion, and operates with its own distinct set of rules and expectations. It is, in many ways, a science as much as an art. Dedicating time and energy to something I'd never done before was exhilarating, but it also brought a unique brand of nerves and vulnerability. Delivering a speech about politics? That's familiar territory—I've made a career of it, armed with the confidence that comes with expertise. But opening up about my personal experiences, offering advice, and sharing insights into what I believe works, was a different challenge. It's one thing to inform; it's another to connect. Learning to do the latter has been humbling and transformative.

There is a certain discomfort in learning a new skill, especially as an adult, and especially when that new skill requires a willingness to be seen and critiqued. I've had to confront my own perfectionism and resist the urge to compare myself to seasoned keynote speakers. I've learned to celebrate small wins—the talk that went a little better than the last, the audience member who reached out to say my story resonated, the moment my nerves settled just enough to let the joy of sharing take hold.

The second Tiny Pivot I've been working on is rooted in my lifelong tendency to get bored quickly. If I'm not challenged, I lose focus, and my productivity wilts. Recognizing this about myself, I sought new opportunities that would push me, that would make me feel a little bit uncomfortable—in a good way. As fate would have it, opportunity knocked in a way I hadn't anticipated. I was approached to provide television commentary, to offer insight and perspective on the election, Capitol Hill, and the Administration.

This was, to put it mildly, nerve-wracking. For one, I had never been on television before. For another, my entire professional training up to that moment had drilled into me a rule: *Never speak to the media.* It felt almost rebellious to say yes—but I said it anyway. I'm glad I did. I discovered that I enjoyed the fast-paced rhythm of live TV, the challenge of developing a succinct point of view on complex issues, and the discipline needed to always be prepared.

Now, I appear on a variety of networks—CNN, Fox Business, Fox News, ABC, CBS, MSNBC, NewsNation, and Bloomberg—each with its own audience and expectations. To do this credibly, I must be informed about a wide range of topics, prepared for on-air debates, and ready to defend my positions. The learning curve is steep, and the feedback can be swift and, at times, brutal. Nothing prepares you for the feeling of being critiqued—not just by viewers at home, but sometimes by colleagues on set or even strangers online. It can be humbling, but it can also be energizing. This Tiny Pivot has forced me to grow, to become sharper, more agile, and more resilient. It has opened new doors and may well be laying the groundwork for future endeavors I haven't even imagined yet.

My third tiny personal pivot is about something far more personal: making sure I truly prioritize and savor every moment my now seventeen-year-old baby, Oliver, wants to spend with me. Watching him grow up so quickly—now learning to drive, testing the boundaries of independence—brings both pride and heartbreak, sometimes all tangled together. Over the last seventeen years, I've logged untold hours driving him to hockey practice, to and from school forty minutes away, and ferrying him between friends, all while juggling the demands of work, travel, and the relentless current of everyday life.

I used to see these car rides as logistical hurdles, puzzle pieces to fit into an already crowded day. Now, I see them as precious windows of time—fleeting opportunities for conversation, for shared music, for comfortable silence, and yes, sometimes for eavesdropping on the animated chatter between Oliver and his friends in the backseat. These moments, so ordinary on the surface, are the ones that matter most. As the prospect of college looms and the reality of losing more time with him sets in, every minute feels golden, and every drive is a memory in the making.

This pivot—toward presence, toward intentionality in my parenting—has put everything else in perspective. My career, my ambitions, even my anxieties, all shrink in the face of the knowledge that these days are numbered. I make it a point to say yes to every opportunity to be with him, to listen, to laugh, and to just be there, knowing that soon, these moments will be rarer and even more precious.

If there's a common thread in all these Tiny Pivots, it's that they are less about radical reinvention and more about continuous, mindful evolution. They are about being honest with myself about what I want, what I need, and where I hope to go—professionally, personally, and as a parent. Growth, I am learning, comes one small pivot at a time. And for now, that is enough.

Business Tiny Pivot

Kristi Remington, Shimmy Stein, Malloy McDaniel, and I started a lobbying firm almost ten years ago. We were looking to be entrepreneurs, to own something after working together at a law firm for several years. The idea came out of my being in business school and thinking we were ready to take the plunge. I remember vividly being in Rio de Janeiro at Fundação Getulio Vargas (FGV), Brazil's partner school to Georgetown that was part of our Master's in Business program. I text messaged the three of them and said, "I'll be home in a few days; let's meet Monday afternoon and put a plan in place to start a firm." Two months later, West Front Strategies was born.

Those first months felt like we were building a ship at sea. None of us had ever started a business from scratch before, and each day brought a new set of challenges and decisions to be made. There was excitement, certainly, but the risk was palpable. What kept us moving forward was an unshakable belief in one another and a shared sense that we could build something both meaningful and enduring.

We had a successful and stable business and, most importantly, liked and respected each other. I'm thankful every day that we took the leap of faith and started something by trusting one another. We had no idea if we would have any clients or whether we would survive. We had a tough time finding a bank that would give us a credit line because we didn't know if we would have any business. One of us even put up a life insurance policy as collateral. I'm proud to say that we only needed our line of credit for three months and were profitable and growing from the start.

Looking back, those early days taught us resilience and the value of measured risk-taking. The hustle was real—calling potential and current clients, leveraging every connection, and navigating Capitol Hill with nothing but our reputations and hoping our clients would take a chance on us. Every existing and new client who put faith in our untested firm strengthened our belief that we had made the right choice.

I'm telling you this because of what comes next. I started getting that feeling that we needed to start planning. We were all getting older and needed to make sure that we had the right people working with us to stay relevant in a town that, in some ways, can be very young. The average age of staffers on Capitol Hill is between twenty-eight and thirty-two years old. We were adding new team members, but the question remained: were we adding enough, and did we need to add even more? At the same time, we were having people and other firms approach us asking to buy the firm.

Something was simmering in my mind, and I needed to start exploring. In 2024, I started the process of meeting with various people who had sold their firms and finding out what it looked like. I read books about how firms made up of "people" as the asset were valued. I had several conversations with other firms of similar size that experienced a comparable situation. In those conversations, I learned the potential pitfalls and benefits that could come from selling the firm.

These meetings were a masterclass in transition—the mechanics of deal structure, the emotional calculus of letting go, and, most importantly, the challenge of integrating teams and cultures. Some stories were cautionary—founders who regretted losing their autonomy, teams that fractured under new management—but others shared tales of renewal and growth, where joining with another firm brought new opportunities and energy. I listened, asked questions, and took copious notes, all while quietly assessing what would work for us.

One night I ran into one of my now partners in a Washington restaurant beside the Capitol. Matt Bravo was at S-3 Group, a firm I'd been collaborating with for years. We shared clients and intelligence, and their leadership, John Scofield and Mike Ference were trusted friends. Others at West Front Strategies were also friends and business associates with various members of the S-3 team. From that brief encounter with Bravo, a seed was planted.

It was a serendipitous meeting that felt almost scripted—two teams with overlapping networks, similar values, and a shared vision for the future of government affairs. During the next several months, our conversations deepened, moving from polite banter to real talk about strategy, culture, and the anxieties that inevitably come with change. I realized that our strengths complemented theirs: where we were scrappy and client-focused, S-3 brought depth in digital communications and a broader bi-partisan reach.

Over the next nine months, we had productive meetings over lunch and at the office. Could a merger between the two firms work? Would the West Front Team be willing to give up our independence and become part of the S-3 team? Did we have too many conflicts? Did we add expertise to each other's respective firms that would make us stronger as one? It became evident that the ultimate answer to all those questions was a confident yes.

Those discussions weren't always easy. We debated everything from leadership structures to compensation models, to the kinds of clients we could and couldn't take. Transparency was key—we laid out our priorities, listened closely to theirs, and tried to surface any potential landmines before the ink was dry. As the months passed, it became clear that the merger wasn't simply about expanding headcount or revenue; it was about building a stronger, more enduring firm that could adapt to the shifting landscape of Washington advocacy.

Now how did we go from making the decision to move forward, to making sure all people at our respective firms were onboard and looking forward to the next phase? This was where the leadership between the two firms would have to work their magic.

In the next chapter, you'll see how I used my Power Pivot for Leadership model to get West Front Strategies where it needed to be as a firm while upholding our core values: hard work and kindness.

Ultimately, this Tiny Pivot—a term that belies the magnitude of what we undertook—became a testament to the power of trust, collaboration, and the willingness to evolve while staying true to who we are.

CHAPTER 14

STRATEGIC TINY PIVOTS DRIVE LASTING LEADERSHIP CHANGE

Even though I had partners at West Front Strategies, I wasn't sure everyone was in the same place as I was with needing a change. I wondered how I was going to convince everyone that making a change was the right strategic thing to do. I'd had a few conversations about the need to grow, but I didn't really have a plan in place. Work was busy, clients were demanding, and our families took priority over making a decisive plan to change.

I started thinking about how to use the Power Pivot for Leadership Framework to help kickstart the tiny Power Pivot we needed to make.

Recognize

I recognized something needed to change, or we wouldn't continue to have the long-term growth we wanted. It was 2024, a major election year with a presidential election and a third of the United States Senate—and the entire House of Representatives—up for grabs. Corporations and companies always get nervous in an election year, wondering if they have the right outside consultant teams in place to be most effective for the next administration and Congress. Truly everyone is at a standstill for about six to nine months as the drama of the election unfolds. It was the right time for the firm to put all the pieces in place and hit the ground running.

Reframe

It became clear that investing in new hires—I was thinking as many as four people—would be risky and success wasn't certain. It would be a time-consuming process to find people that fit our culture and values. Then the time invested in training them would take an incredible amount of energy. Yes, I wanted to find people who would flourish in our boutique firm, but I wasn't sure I had the time and motivation to do it. I've built several organizations over the years, and it is tough, time-consuming work with no guarantees.

Selling West Front Strategies also came with uncertainty. I did lots of research by talking to people who'd been through it, and by reading everything I could get my hands on to find out the success rate of firms such as ours being bought by another firm or a private equity company. There was no guarantee that the model worked, and there is always a buyout period that can be long (four to five years). It can profoundly change the foundation of a small firm. You go from working and managing your own success and failures to working for someone else and managing to their revenue and bottom lines. There had been some success with this model, but I didn't see my partners or myself being ready to lose that much control of what we started.

I realized that, at its core, the reframe stage is about challenging assumptions—both my own and those that had become ingrained in the firm's DNA. We had always prided ourselves on being agile and close-knit, qualities that larger organizations often envy. But agility comes with its own set of vulnerabilities, particularly as client expectations shift and market pressures intensify. I began to see our options not as either-or choices, but as invitations to think deeper about the kind of firm we wanted to be: one that reacts to change, or one that anticipates it and moves proactively.

Finally, the idea of merging with another firm was seeming much more appealing. The key was doing it with the right people.

Redirect

The managing partner of S-3 Group, John Scofield, as I've mentioned, was a friend for many years. The two of us, along with Mike Ference, the other majority shareholder at S-3, began having conversations around what a merger could look like. We talked about and pondered each other's strengths, and the gaps that we each had. We looked at our client lists to determine conflicts that hypothetically couldn't be mitigated, and we talked in detail about the culture of the two firms and whether the two groups of people could work together towards a common goal: building an even bigger, better firm than what the two firms already had. We thought the merger could work, and we had a lot of reasons to believe it could be *great*. Now came the hard part: selling it to everyone else involved.

Over many conversations, lunches, drinks, and laughter, the partners of the two firms came to a joint conclusion to give it a go. Over several months we set up everything to transition our firm into theirs. We worked through tough conversations, like how we would share equity, and we conferred with our clients, who were very supportive of the potential merger.

Finally, we were ready to announce the new entity.

At the end of October 2024, we did just that. We announced that West Front Strategies and S-3 Group were merging several weeks before Election Day, as none of us wanted to make significant decisions based on the outcome of any election. We wanted to have a solid bi-partisan firm that would be successful no matter who won. As I write this book, we are through the first year of the merger, and it has been wildly successful. We've been able to service our clients better than we did before, and we see revenue growing expediently. Most importantly, we all like and respect each other.

I call the example I just walked through a "Tiny Pivot" and not a "Power Pivot" because even though the merger did change all our lives, I would argue—for the better—that it wasn't a *complete* life change for me. It was just another change intended to set me on the trajectory of my next Power Pivot.

Tiny Pivots are important as big decisions are made. It takes some of the fear and risk out of a major life change. They can also make certain parts of your life manageable if the timing isn't right for a major life change. If you make a slight change and it doesn't work, it is easier to get back on track before you make a mistake that is too big or could take a long time to reverse. Here are some thoughts on why these "Tiny Pivots" are so important and integral to the Power Pivot journey.

They:

- **Build Momentum.** Big changes can feel daunting. Tiny Pivots break the journey into manageable steps, creating early wins that boost confidence and motivation.
- **Reduce Overwhelming Emotions.** By focusing on small actions, you avoid paralysis brought on by the scale of the Power Pivot.
- **Create Habits.** Consistent Tiny Pivots form new habits that support the larger change. For example, getting up at 5:00 AM consistently creates a structure conducive to accomplishment.
- **Allow Experimentation.** Tiny Pivots let you test strategies on a small scale, learning what works before committing fully.
- **Foster Resilience.** Small setbacks are easier to recover from, keeping you on track toward the Power Pivot.
- **Compound Over Time.** The more "Tiny Pivots" you make, the more they accumulate, leading to considerable progress.

But the real power of a Tiny Pivot, I've discovered, is its capacity to empower leaders—and organizations—to stay nimble amid uncertainty. Rather than waiting for a perfect moment or an overwhelming sense of clarity, you move, you experiment, and you adjust. Tiny Pivots allow you to build a culture of adaptability, where change isn't something to fear or resist, but something to embrace as a natural part of growth.

In the months following the merger, we found that these small, deliberate adjustments in how we conducted team meetings, onboarded clients, and checked in with one another had an outsized impact. They paved the way for bigger shifts and for a new collective identity that was stronger than the sum of its parts.

Now the question is: How do you incorporate the changes you're making into your broader Power Pivot?

These are examples of what I've used to make my Tiny Pivots effective:

- ***Align with Your Why.*** Ensure each Tiny Pivot ties directly to your overarching Power Pivot goal to keep focus.
- ***Start Small.*** Choose actions so easy you can't fail. (For example, "read one page" instead of "read a book.")
- ***Use Triggers.*** Pair Tiny Pivots with existing habits. (For example, meditating for two minutes after brushing your teeth.)
- ***Stay Flexible.*** If a Tiny Pivot isn't working, tweak it rather than abandoning the entire goal.
- ***Leverage Community.*** Share your Tiny Pivots with a friend or group for accountability. (For example, you could post your progress on social media or tell friends your goal and how you are doing.)

It's important to remember that Tiny Pivots are not about settling for less—they're about making progress visible and sustainable. The satisfaction of progress, no matter how incremental, generates more momentum for the next step.

Tiny Pivots are the building blocks of a successful Power Pivot. They transform a daunting, abstract goal into a series of concrete, achievable steps. By consistently taking these small actions, you create a sustainable path to change, avoid burnout, and build the confidence needed to fully embrace the larger shift.

The journey of leadership isn't defined by a handful of monumental moments, but rather by the accumulation of these small, pivotal choices. Each Tiny Pivot, while seemingly insignificant by themselves, lays the foundation for transformation. Embrace them; celebrate their wins and learn from their failures. Over time, you'll look back and see how these modest steps have propelled you further than you ever imagined possible.

EPILOGUE

THE ART OF THE POWER PIVOT: EMBRACING CHANGE WITH PURPOSE AND VISION

Change is the only constant in life, yet so often, we fear it, resist it, or dismiss its potential. The term "pivot" has become ubiquitous in the worlds of personal and professional development, and it signifies a conscious and strategic shift in direction. A Power Pivot is all that and more. It's more than a change—it's an *intentional* rerouting in response to new information, self-awareness, or changing circumstances.

Being intentional empowers us to pursue meaningful change with clarity and conviction. And if we expect success, we must start with the understanding that it isn't just a destination. Success is the outcome of consistent, deliberate action. If we truly expect to reach it, we must embrace the discipline, resilience, and dedication the process demands—and above all, we must take full ownership of the steps within our control.

I've made a compelling case for the transformative force behind the Power Pivot. Whether pursuing a career goal, like a promotion, or working toward a personal goal, such as improved health, real change begins with clarity. It demands that we define specific, actionable steps and follow through with unshakable intention. When we do, we don't just adapt to the moment—we reorient our trajectory toward something far more powerful: lasting growth.

Embracing change and pivoting with purpose isn't just transformative; it's catalytic and can change your life, enhance your career, and reinvigorate your business. It certainly did for me, and it will for you—if you have the courage to self-reflect, plan strategically, and take bold action. Power Pivots can turn uncertainty into opportunity and stagnation into growth.

I walked you through the three types of Power Pivots—Personal, Business, and Leadership—each of which share common traits but also include plans of action unique to them.

Personal Power Pivots: Embracing Growth at Every Turn

A meaningful Personal Power Pivot begins with introspection, the courageous act of turning inward to find areas ripe for change. These pivots often require that we confront fears in their many forms—fear of the unknown, fear of judgment, or fear of failure. Yet, when we choose to reframe fear not as a warning sign, but as an indicator of where potential growth is possible, something remarkable happens. We unlock doors to new experiences, forge deeper relationships, and set the stage for achievements that once felt out of reach.

Consider the individual who, midway through their career, recognizes they've outgrown their role or industry. Rather than interpreting this discomfort as failure, they honor it as an internal prompt—a signal that greater fulfillment lies elsewhere. This realization sparks a journey of introspection and recalibration, where they assess their values, strengths, and aspirations with fresh clarity. With courage, they pivot into a new field aligned with who they've become, not just what they've done. And while the terrain ahead may be unfamiliar, it's often where the most meaningful chapters begin—full of energy, purpose, and renewed excitement. A quick recap of what we learned:

Framework for Personal Pivots:

- **Self-Assessment.** Use tools like journaling, personality assessments, or feedback from trusted peers to clarify what you want and what's holding you back.
- **Vision Setting.** Visualize your desired future and set clear, incremental goals that build momentum.
- **Skill Acquisition.** Identify necessary skills or knowledge gaps and create a plan to bridge them.
- **Action and Reflection.** Make small, consistent actions and regularly reflect on progress, lessons, and adjustments needed.

Resilience is a cornerstone of successful pivots. Building it means cultivating a growth mindset, embracing uncertainty, and viewing setbacks as learning opportunities rather than permanent failures. Those who adapt and push through a setback are more likely to find fulfillment in their new directions and achieve their goals.

If the goal is to pivot into a new career, it's usually prompted by a desire for advancement, job satisfaction, or a better alignment with your personal values. To be successful with that pivot, you begin with research and networking. Identify industries or roles that excite you, reach out to professionals in those fields, and seek mentorship. Take courses, certifications, or on-the-job training to further your knowledge. Go back to college—I did. These pivots can rekindle passion and motivation, reduce burnout, and lead to roles that better fit what you want. By confidently steering your pivot, you take ownership of your happiness and success.

Think of the teacher who transitions into corporate training, the marketer who moves to non-profit work, or the engineer who launches a startup. Each story begins with curiosity and is powered by proactive steps: informational interviews, skill-building, and the humility to start fresh.

Action Steps:

- Map your transferable skills and highlight their relevance to your target industry.
- Build a network in your new field—attend events, join online communities, and seek guidance from those who've made similar transitions.
- Experiment with side projects, volunteering, or freelance work to gain hands-on experience and credibility.

Business Power Pivots: Innovate, Adapt, Thrive

The Business Power Pivot is born from the need to remain relevant and competitive. The most iconic business stories—from Netflix's shift from DVDs to streaming, to YouTube's transformation from a dating site to a video platform—are tales of bold pivots in the face of changing market realities. Successful business pivots require visionary leadership, clear communication, and a willingness to take calculated risks. Engaging teams in the pivot process, listening to employees and customers, and staying transparent about challenges and goals fosters buy-in and resilience.

Framework for Business Pivots:

- **Market Awareness.** Regularly scan the environment for trends, threats, and emerging opportunities.
- **Open Dialogue.** Foster a culture where employees feel safe to propose new ideas and challenge the status quo.
- **Constant Action.** Use pilot programs and test markets to confirm new directions before a full commitment.
- **Agile Leadership.** Empower teams to adapt quickly, learn from failures, and iterate toward success.

In business, Power Pivots are essential for longevity. Markets shift. Technologies evolve. Customer needs change. Companies that do not adapt risk irrelevance. Remember, strategic pivots don't signal failure; they show agility. Leaders who embrace pivots foster cultures of innovation, learning, and long-term growth. They see change not as a threat, but as an opportunity to reimagine what's possible.

Leadership Power Pivots: Leading the Charge with Vision

Which leads me to the Leadership Power Pivot. Leaders must remain vigilant, constantly scanning the horizon for emerging opportunities and threats. The most successful leaders are not those who avoid change, but those who embrace it intentionally, strategically, and decisively. Unlike reactive changes or panic-driven decisions, a Leadership Power Pivot is a purposeful and value-driven shift that realigns business strategy with vision, opportunity, and evolving market realities. For business leaders, mastering the art of the Power Pivot is not just a skill—it's a necessity for long-term relevance, resilience, and growth.

Leadership Power Pivots aren't just business decisions—they're leadership moments. They require courage to disrupt the status quo, a clarity of vision, and empathy to bring others along.

Framework for Leadership:

- Model adaptability to build a culture of change-readiness.
- Communicate with transparency to maintain trust.
- Inspire with vision, especially when navigating ambiguity.

By owning the narrative and purpose behind the pivot, leaders can turn uncertainty into a unifying force that energizes teams and renews organizational momentum.

Consider Satya Nadella's transformation of Microsoft's culture from "know-it-all" to "learn-it-all," or Howard Schultz's return to Starbucks during crisis. These leaders didn't just change the company's direction—they galvanized people with purpose and clear, authentic communication.

The modern business landscape demands leaders who can effectively pivot. A well-executed Power Pivot is a strategic reset, allowing leaders to turn disruption into direction and stagnation into growth. By embracing this mindset and process, business leaders position themselves—and their organizations—not just to survive change, but to lead it.

The Psychology of Pivoting: Overcoming Barriers

Despite the potential of Power Pivots, fear and uncertainty can paralyze action. Our brains are wired for familiarity; we find comfort in the known, even if it's unfulfilling. The key is to practice self-compassion and recognize that discomfort is a signpost, not a stop sign. Seek support from mentors, friends, or coaches. Break substantial changes into manageable steps and celebrate each milestone.

Actionable Advice for Lasting Change:

- Start with small, reversible changes before committing to a full pivot.
- Surround yourself with a supportive community that encourages experimentation and growth.
- Document your process—journaling can reveal patterns, boost accountability, and clarify your journey.
- Continually revisit your values and vision to ensure your pivot stays aligned with what matters most.

Embracing the Power Pivot Mindset

Remember, whether in personal choices, career shifts, or business strategies, the power of a pivot lies in its capacity to turn uncertainty into possibility. When done with purpose and intention, a Power Pivot can be the most transformative decision you ever make. Rather than fearing change, we must learn to embrace it as a strategic opportunity to realign with our goals and evolve into the next—and better—version of ourselves, our businesses, and our careers.

The journey of a thousand pivots begins with a single, intentional step. The question isn't if change will come, but whether you will meet it with resistance or with the courage, vision, and resilience that a Power Pivot demands. If you choose the latter, you'll transform not just your path, but yourself.

ACKNOWLEDGMENTS

When you've been in the political world for as long as I have, you inevitably develop a thick skin so hard that it stops being solely protective and starts shaping how you live your life. Trusting people is always complicated. There is a saying in Washington that we are always one day away from being on the front page. It's a fitting reminder of how quickly the tides can turn in public life. I have refused to let this high-stakes cutthroat environment shape my identity. Instead, I've anchored myself in the support of my family and a trusted inner circle of people who remind me who I am beyond the headlines.

Mom and Dad...thank you from the bottom of my heart. You support and encourage me to do whatever I put my mind to. From when I was a little girl in gymnastics, to a young adult moving Harrisburg, Pennsylvania for the first time, you have always told me you are proud of whatever I am doing and give soft advice to send me in the right direction. I could not have had two better parents to show me the way.

To my brother, Jason, thank you for letting me be the annoying little sister who was always pushing the envelope and driving you crazy. You are an amazing dad and husband, and I could not be prouder of who you are.

Sam and Kara—well, we have been through it all. Friends for literally fifty years, from sitting on Santa's lap together, to experiencing boyfriends, parties, tattoos, heartbreak, husbands, and babies, who are growing lightning fast. You are sisters to me, and I cherish every minute we had and will have together.

Over the course of my nearly thirty-year career, I have had the privilege of working alongside—and learning from—remarkable leaders. Ironically, every one of my greatest mentors has been a man who generously took me under his wing and taught me the ropes across areas like lobbying, government, law firms, investments, and life itself. To my beloved Bill Greenlee, who is no longer with us, Stan Rapp, Governor Tom Ridge, Hector Irastorza, Mike Dyer, David Girard-diCarlo, and Bob Mittman—thank you.

Julie, Aimee, Sara, Emily and Colleen, Mel, and Heather—from meeting in 2000 on President Bush's first campaign to living in Washington for the twenty-five years since, it has been a ride. Through the chaos, calm, politics, and whirlwind of the "swamp," you have been my anchors. The one constant that I've always counted on is knowing you have my back. I am not sure I would have survived all of these years if I hadn't been able to call on you for our "4:00 PM meetings." Thank you—for your loyalty, your friendship, and the unwavering support that has carried me through every chapter.

Kristi Remington, Malloy McDaniel, and Shimmy Stein, you have been through most of my professional pivots with me, from our days at Blank Rome, to West Front Strategies, and now S-3 Group. Thank you for sticking with my crazy ideas and taking chances with me, from my text from Brazil saying, *"We're starting a firm, who's in?!,"* to merging with S-3 Group ten years later to ensure we were growing and thriving with colleagues we now and trust.

To my agent, Stephanie Cassidy who pushed me to turn my speech into a book and connected me with Post Hill Press to make this a reality.

Dave Erickson…I couldn't have done it without you. My strength is not writing, and you challenged me to get to where I needed to be. And of course, Mira Adwell Photography, who made me look at least five years younger.

Finally, I want to express my dearest thanks to Oliver and Joel. For more than twenty years, Joel and I have ridden this life through ups and downs that life throws at us. We created an insanely amazing human being in Oliver and have raised him together to be an amazing young man. Joel is the true writer in the family and helped me every step through this process. Thank you for sticking with me through all my pivots, mostly good, some challenging—and I know it won't surprise anyone who reads this book that I can be a little difficult sometimes.

Oliver, you truly are the best thing that has ever happened to me. I always worried that as a working mom you would resent the times that I have been away or worked late. But when I look at the kind, gentle, smart, adorable human you have become, it shows me I have done something right. I know you have such a bright future, and I can't wait to watch you continue to grow. I love you, my baby.